SINGLE MAN WALKING through DIVORCE

Healing, Faith, And Strength For The Journey Through And After Divorce

GEORGE LAMELZA

Single Man Walking Through Divorce

Copyright © 2026 Single Christianity LLC
All rights reserved.

No part of this book may be reproduced or transmitted in any form or by any means, electronic or mechanical, including photocopying, recording, or by any information storage and retrieval system, without prior written permission from the publisher, except for brief quotations in reviews.

Written by George Lamelza.
Published by Single Christianity LLC.

Printed in the United States of America.

For more information or to book an event, visit:
https://www.singlemanwalking.com

Most names and identifying details in this book have been changed to protect the privacy of the individuals involved. Any resemblance to actual persons, living or dead, is coincidental.

Disclaimer

This book is based on the author's personal experiences, reflections, and faith journey. It is intended for informational and inspirational purposes only and is not a substitute for professional counseling, legal, medical, or financial advice. The author is not a licensed counselor, therapist, or legal professional. Readers are encouraged to seek guidance from qualified professionals regarding mental health, divorce recovery, financial matters, or legal concerns. Every person's journey is unique, and the insights shared reflect the author's personal process and experience.

Scripture quotations are primarily taken from the Holy Bible, New International Version® (NIV®), Copyright © 1973, 1978, 1984, 2011 by Biblica, Inc.® Used by permission. All rights reserved worldwide. www.zondervan.com. The "NIV" and "New International Version" are registered trademarks of Biblica, Inc.®. Some quotations are from the English Standard Version® (ESV®), Copyright © 2001 by Crossway, a publishing ministry of Good News Publishers. Used by permission. All rights reserved. www.crossway.org. Other Scripture quotations are adapted by the author for conversational clarity.

ISBN (Paperback): 979-8-9945218-0-9
ISBN (eBook): 979-8-9945218-1-6
ISBN (Audiobook): 979-8-9945218-2-3

First Edition: 2026

PREFACE

In a world where information is cheap and everywhere, the only thing we truly own is our story.

The real story—the one we actually lived. The one that carries the scars and the strength.

You can find a video to fix a car, use AI to search for all the answers, and follow step-by-step guides for almost anything. But for all that closeness to knowledge, we've never been more disconnected. And then comes divorce—hailed in some corners of our culture as "freedom"—but leaving consequences that can stretch for years.

For me, it didn't just rearrange my living situation or my bank account. Divorce shook my identity, tested my faith, and forced me to face questions I never thought I'd have to ask:

Who am I now?
Where is God in all this?
How do I move forward when the life I built is gone?

I didn't figure it out quickly. I wandered. I stumbled. I resisted. I tried to rush healing, patching the holes with distractions—work, relationships, money, anything that could make it look like I was fine. But eventually, the truth caught up. That's when the real journey began.

This book isn't about quick fixes or easy answers. It's about the long road. It's about what happened when I stopped pretending, took an honest look at my life, and finally invited God into the mess. It's about learning to rebuild from the inside out—spiritually, emotionally, physically, and financially—because if even one of those is left in ruins, the rest will eventually crumble.

If you're holding this book, you might be at the very start of that road. Or maybe you're somewhere in the middle. Or maybe it's been years since your divorce, but you can still feel its weight. Wherever you are, I want you to know this: God's not finished with you. The same grace that met me in my lowest moments is available to you right now.

You won't find a formula here, but you will find a companion for the journey—a raw, honest look at failure, faith, and the slow, sometimes painful, work of becoming whole again.

If you're willing to walk this road with me, I believe you'll discover what I did: healing doesn't happen all at once, but it does happen. And the life on the other side can be richer, stronger, and more meaningful than you ever imagined.

CONTENTS

Chapter 01. Starting Over - A New Life Begins................. 7
Chapter 02. Don't Be Me. Here's Why.. 15
Chapter 03. Facing the Emotional Storm 21
Chapter 04. The Emotional Anchor - Finding Safe Harbor in the Storm .29
Chapter 05. The Stages of Divorce Recovery 39
Chapter 06. A Year of Healing - My Divorce Journey 49
Chapter 07. Walking Through Loneliness With Strength 59
Chapter 08. Reclaiming Your Identity After Divorce.. 67
Chapter 09. Letting God Defend Your Name.. 73
Chapter 10. Forgiveness - The Hardest, Most Important Step 81
Chapter 11. Fatherhood After Divorce - Loving Your Kids Well.. ...89
Chapter 12. Talking to Your Ex Without Conflict 97
Chapter 13. The Financial Storm - The Collapse That Saved Me. ..103
Chapter 14. Dating Again - When Healing Comes First.. 113
Chapter 15. The Line in the Sand....................... 123
Chapter 16. Choosing Purity After Failure 131
Chapter 17. Remarriage - God's Timing & Your Calling 143
Chapter 18. Walking Into Your Next Chapter 153

Acknowledgments.. 159
About the Author. 161

CHAPTER
01
STARTING OVER
A NEW LIFE BEGINS

"For the past ten years, I lived a life most people dream about: a beautiful wife, amazing kids, the best job, and financial freedom. Every part of it looked like perfection. From the outside, we had what everyone wanted—and in my heart, I believed we did too.

Now it's all gone."

That was the first entry in my journal after my marriage ended—a journal I filled with pain, confusion, questions, and eventually, the slow return of hope.

Divorce didn't just break a promise. It shattered the entire framework I had built my life around. It wasn't just a relational loss—it was the unraveling of my identity as a man, a husband, a father, and a provider. Everything I thought was secure… was gone.

And underneath it all was one thing: **fear**.

Fear I'd lose everything.
Fear I'd never love again.
Fear I'd never be whole again.
Fear I'd always be this broken version of myself.

What I Did Instead of Healing

After the divorce, I didn't take time to grieve. I went into overdrive.

I dated. I chased. I hustled. I partied. I drank too much. I filled every moment in my life with something—anything—that looked like success, connection, or purpose. I wasn't just looking for love. I was looking to be seen by someone—anyone—because deep down, I didn't even recognize myself.

I poured myself into people, into work, into trying to prove that I was okay.

I went from leading a thriving company to losing it all—my business, my home, and eventually, the identity I had clung to. But none of it filled the kind of emptiness you can't cover with busyness or distractions.

It was deeper than that.

What I didn't realize was that I wasn't just grieving the loss of my marriage. I was carrying wounds I had never dealt with—some going all the way back to my childhood.

Instability. Homelessness. A secret addiction to pornography. The shame of adultery in my marriage. I had buried it all under achievement, performance, and a smile.

And now, with nothing left to stand on, it all came crashing in.

I kept trying to be the "strong, successful guy." But I didn't feel strong.

I felt broken.
I felt lost. Angry. Embarrassed. Abandoned. Confused. Ashamed. Forgotten.

And above all else—afraid.

What Do You Do When You Lose Everything?

When your world falls apart, you learn who you really are.

It's easy to look put together when life is going your way. But when everything gets stripped away, what's left?

That question haunted me:

Who am I now?

I tried to keep up appearances. I kept showing up for my kids. I kept showing up at church. I even led a divorce group for over five years, helping others find healing—but I kept putting

mine off.
I smiled when people needed me to smile.
But the truth was—I was barely holding it together.

Eventually, pretending stopped working.

I needed help.
Real help.

Counseling.
Conversations with people who didn't sugarcoat the truth.
Friends who would sit in the mess with me and not try to fix it.

And most of all, I needed to face the one relationship I had been avoiding for years: **my relationship with God**.

Honest Enough to Begin

I didn't come back to God with a polished prayer or bold faith.

I wasn't kneeling at an altar.
I was in my car. Alone.
Parked outside a church I couldn't even bring myself to walk into.

I just sat there.
Staring at the dashboard.

My hands gripping the steering wheel like it could somehow hold me together.

I didn't have answers. I didn't have clarity. I didn't even know what I believed anymore.

All I could whisper was,

"I need You, God. Help me."

Not a powerful prayer. Not a faith-filled declaration.
Just a quiet, broken honesty from someone who had nothing left to give.

And in that silence—I didn't hear a voice. Nothing miraculous happened around me.

But something in me shifted after I got out of the car, and finally walked into church.

It wasn't clarity.
It was surrender.

I stopped fighting.
I stopped trying to manage the pain.

I just let it be what it was—grief, shame, regret, longing, confusion, all of it—and let God meet me there.

That whisper was the first honest thing I had said in a long time.

That moment of honesty cracked the door open to real healing.

The reality is that healing did not come quickly or cleanly. There were nights I cried myself to sleep.

I stared at the ceiling in the mornings, wishing I could stay in bed.

Moments, I felt like I had failed everyone—my kids, God, and myself.

Starting over was not one big decision or some emotional breakthrough.

It was an intentional choice.

Small, hard steps, one after another—most of them feeling like they led nowhere.

I wasn't trying to be strong.
I was just trying to survive.
Because surviving was all I ever knew.

That is how I grew up—always in survival mode, never really living, just making it to the next day.

Little by little, though—through prayer, Scripture, and some brutally honest conversations—I realized something.

God never left me.

Even when I tried to leave Him.

And that truth—slowly, quietly—began to change me.

The Big Four

From there, I began to rebuild. Slowly. Imperfectly. But with intention.

I focused on what I now call the Big Four—I realized that they were essential, not just for surviving, but for becoming healthy, whole, and healed:

- **Spiritual health** — I had to reconnect with God for real, not just show up on Sundays.
- **Emotional health** — I had to stop numbing and start feeling.
- **Physical health** — I had to care for my body and rebuild discipline.
- **Financial health** — I had to own where I was and rebuild with integrity.

You'll see these woven throughout the book, because they shaped every stage of my journey toward becoming the man I was meant to be.

What This Book Will Give You

This isn't a book with all the answers.
I'm just telling my story.

Each chapter will include real stories—hard-earned lessons I've lived, not just ideas or theories.

At the end of each chapter, you'll find three things designed to help you keep moving forward:

- **Reflection questions** — A few prompts to help you be honest about where you are.

- **A practical activity** — Something simple that helped me take a step when I felt stuck.

- **A prayer** — Because even when I didn't know what to say, speaking anything to God mattered.

You don't have to do it perfectly.
You don't have to have it all figured out.

This isn't about crossing a finish line.
It's about taking the next step—one honest moment at a time.

CHAPTER
02
DON'T BE ME. HERE'S WHY.

We live in a world obsessed with speed. Coffee in two minutes. Groceries in an hour. Answers instantly. And when you're going through a divorce, that urgency multiplies. Every emotion gets louder. Every task feels heavier. Life falls apart in slow motion, and your brain screams, Fix this. Now.

I get it. I didn't want to sit in it either. I didn't want advice. I didn't want books. I didn't want to feel. I just wanted it to stop hurting. I wanted clarity, direction—something to make it all make sense.

But pain doesn't go away just because you want it to. I learned that the hard way. Wanting without doing kept me stuck. And being stuck eventually became familiar. Comfortable, even. It was easier to numb out than face the wreckage.

So this chapter isn't a list of dos and don'ts because I figured it all out. It's here because I didn't. And if someone had handed me something like this back then, I probably wouldn't have listened to all of it. But maybe I would've listened to a few things.

What follows is the stripped-down version—for the guy who doesn't want to read a hundred pages before something hits. These are the things that helped me heal… or made things worse when I ignored them.

Take what helps. Leave what doesn't.

But now at least, you'll know.

Top 10 DO's While Going Through Divorce

1. **Find a mentor.**

    Plain and simple, you need other men in your life. Not buddies who tell you what you want to hear—someone who's walked through hard things and can speak into your life.

When I finally settled into the reality that I didn't know everything, and submitted my pride, I was able to hear someone other than my own distorted voice.

2. **Get counseling.**

   A good counselor gives you space to let it all out without being judged or fixed. I could just sit and be raw—no hiding, no performing. The real me at that time was hurting and acting out in all the wrong ways.

3. **Find a hobby.**

   Ride bikes, build something, take a photography class, or do something that gets you out of your head. I started writing—just dumping everything out—and it became a healthy outlet.

4. **Work out.**

   Move your body three or four times a week, even if it's just for thirty minutes. It shifts everything. My perspective changed when I started doing this consistently.

5. **Serve someone else.**

   Volunteer somewhere. Find a place where you're not the center. I served at a local charity. Honestly, I dreaded going every time—but once I was there, I felt alive again.

6. **Go somewhere safe.**

   When in doubt, go to a coffee shop. Sit. Read. People-watch. I closed down Barnes & Noble three nights a week to avoid being alone in the house.

7. **Journal everything.**

   Even if it feels stupid, write it down. It gave my pain somewhere to go. I started by writing what I thought people wanted to hear—but over time, the real stuff came out. That's where the healing began.

8. **Pick a theme song.**

    Music helped me survive. I had a different song every few months—something that gave me strength through court, hard conversations, or just the days I didn't want to get out of bed.

9. **Speak life over yourself.**

    Say God's truth—even when you don't feel it. I'd say things like: *I am forgiven (Ephesians 1:7). I am loved (Romans 5:8). I have a great future (Philippians 3:20). I am victorious (1 Corinthians 15:57).* It felt fake at first, but over time, those words started to reshape me.

10. **Pray. Pray. Pray.**

    You don't need fancy words. Just talk. You'll see prayers at the end of each of the following chapters—things that helped me when I didn't know how or what to speak.

Of course, doing the right things helps.

But avoiding the wrong ones? That will save you even more pain.

Top 10 DON'TS While Going Through Divorce

1. **Don't start a new romantic relationship.**

    When I was single again, I wasn't myself—I was "Super George." Heightened emotions, total performance. If she needed funny, I was funny. If she wanted driven, I was driven. Until I wasn't. Dating didn't fix it. Sex didn't heal it. I wasn't the exception to the rule.

2. **Don't party your way through it.**

    The high fades. The crash always comes. I passed out in cars, in places I didn't know, with people I barely remembered. The next morning always felt worse.

3. **Don't hang around negative people.**

    One toxic word can throw your peace, even from family and friends. They meant well, but sometimes their blame-shifting just messed with my head. I had to learn how to love them from a distance.

4. **Don't talk trash about your ex.**

    Especially around your kids. They don't need your adult feelings dumped on their childhood. I remembered how my parents did that—and I made the decision early: I wouldn't do that to mine.

5. **Don't use your kids as leverage.**

    Trying to hurt your ex through your kids will only hurt them. I've watched it happen for decades. The kids carry the pain long after the court orders end.

6. **Don't blow through money.**

    Don't be the "Disney Dad" or the "high roller." I threw away thousands—on trips to happening places, on bar tabs for strangers—to feel powerful again. But the consequences stuck around for years.

7. **Don't make your divorce your personality.**

    People can only hear the same story so many times. Even close friends will start to pull back. I had to find other ways—counseling, journaling—to process my pain without turning every conversation into a therapy session.

8. **Don't go extreme on anything.**

    Work, play, food, sleep—none of it can heal you. I used both partying and work as my escape. It took years to let go.

9. **Don't check up on your ex.**

    No social media stalking. No asking mutual friends. I learned fast: there are things I was better off not knowing.

10. **Don't make major life decisions.**

    Only do what you need to do to protect yourself, your children (if you have them), and your finances. I made big decisions early—driven by pride and emotion—and I paid for them later.

I could give you twenty more. But these? These are the ones I lived.

You don't have to follow them perfectly. I didn't.
But these words come from real scars.

The goal isn't to get through this fast.
The goal is to walk through it whole.

Most guys remarry—most of those end in divorce again.
If you want to repeat the cycle, ignore the list.

But if you want something better—something real, something whole—this is a good place to start.

CHAPTER 03
FACING THE EMOTIONAL STORM

On March 21, 2003, the world watched in real-time as the United States launched a bombing campaign over Iraq—an operation the media quickly labeled "shock and awe." Explosions lit up the night sky, broadcast into living rooms around the world. It looked fast. Precise. Powerful.

But what followed wasn't quick at all. The campaign may have been launched in a moment, but rebuilding would take years.

Divorce is kind of like that.

Your whole world gets torn down in an instant. But rebuilding? That's the part no one shows in slow motion. That's the part I wasn't prepared for.

My Shock & Awe

It was July 13, 2003. A beautiful Sunday in Orlando, Florida. I'd spent five days there with one of my best childhood friends. It was the kind of guy time I hadn't had in years—carefree, easy, full of laughter.

I'm a reflective traveler. Being away from home gives me space to zoom out, to appreciate everything I have. On the plane back to Missouri, I remember looking out the window thinking, *I've made it.* I had a successful business, two beautiful daughters, a strong marriage (or so I thought), great friends, and financial freedom. Everything felt like it was finally clicking.

By the time the flight landed, everything had changed.

That night, after the girls were in bed, my wife sat me down and said four words that detonated my world:

"I want a divorce."

There wasn't an argument. No shouting match. Just a quiet statement that sliced straight through. And I knew—this wasn't a conversation. It was a conclusion.

I begged. I pleaded. But the decision was already made.

I walked down to the basement that night in shock, curled up on a spare bed, and wept until breathing felt impossible. The days that followed were a blur. I was numb. Frozen. Everything I'd built, everything I trusted, was slipping through my fingers.

I didn't know where to start. I didn't want to start.

Trying to Feel Normal Again

I didn't want rules. I didn't want religion. The church's version of "care" felt more like judgment. Friends said things like, "You're young. You'll bounce back," or "Everybody gets divorced now," or worse, "You made your bed, now lie in it."

All I wanted was for the pain to stop.

But nothing felt right. Nothing tasted, smelled, or sounded the same. I'd swing between total control and total collapse. I'd sleep for days or not at all. I was spiraling.

And still—nobody really saw it. I kept showing up and smiling when I needed to. But inside, I was wrecked. I had no idea how to rebuild from the rubble.

And I didn't want to deal with any of it.

Where's the Party At?

Not long after moving to a new home, I met my new neighbor, standing at the edge of our driveways.

"My wife just left me," he said.

And with that, we became instant friends. Bonded by brokenness.

We didn't want healing. We wanted escape. So, we created our own version of divorce recovery: keep partying until life makes sense.

The party crowd didn't need explanations. They didn't care if I went to church or what I'd done. Religion kept asking if I was the guilty or innocent party. The crowd asked, "Who's buying the next round?"

At night, I'd wrap myself in music, alcohol, and female attention. I tried to bury the man I used to be. But the emptiness never left. I was still so broken.

The First Crack

One Saturday night, I left the party early. Something hit me—quiet, unexpected.

I had been looking around the room, watching people drink, dance, and laugh. But it was like watching a movie in slow motion. Every smile looked forced. Every conversation felt hollow. It hit me that I wasn't the only one trying to feel okay. We were all just floating in a room full of noise, numbing whatever we didn't want to name.

I drove home in silence. No music. No calls. Just me and the weight of it all.

I thought about the story of the prodigal son. Not because I was ready to come home. But because something in me wanted to want to.

I remember kneeling beside my bed, whispering something like, "God, if You're there... I need You."

Not Yet Ready

But let's be honest: That didn't change anything.

I wanted help, but I didn't want to do the work. I wanted peace, but I didn't want to let go of comfort. I said the words, but I wasn't ready to live them.

That became my pattern post-divorce—professing one thing in pain but returning to what was easy the moment the pain dulled.

The party still felt good. The affirmation from women still felt good. Feeling like a big deal still felt good. The sin still felt good.

I didn't want to change—I just wanted the pain to go away.

But that whisper? That small cry? It was still a crack in the wall I had built.

And sometimes, that's how real change begins. Not with resolve. Not with repentance. But with a whisper. A small crack in the narrative, I kept telling myself. A moment of honesty that didn't fix me but exposed the lie that what I was doing wasn't working.

Now that I knew the lie, it got harder to pretend.

Living in the Tension

So began the next decade of living a double life. I lived in tension between the man I wanted to become and the one I couldn't seem to let go of. Part of me wanted freedom, peace, and healing. But I also wanted it to be easy.

I treated healing like people treat the gym in January—full of hope on day one, but ready to quit by day two when there's no front-row parking.

So, I started to try church. I'd show up on Sunday mornings still smelling like the night before, hoping for something to stick. I'd hear a sermon and think about doing something—but then go home to my comfort, my habits, my pain-numbing rituals.

I'd open my Bible... sometimes. I'd pray, usually after making another mistake. I thought about changing—really changing—but didn't. Not fully. Not yet.

I cycled through this for years. Moments of clarity. Moments of hope. But the problem was—I got comfortable, even in the chaos. Not because it felt good, but because it felt familiar.

And comfort, even in dysfunction, asked nothing of me. It lulled me into accepting that numb was normal. That this is just how life is going to feel. That the best was behind me.

Comfort Kills

Comfort was the real killer. It killed hope. It killed peace. It killed tomorrow. And it shook me when I finally saw it for what it was.

In those moments when the mask slipped, when the silence got too loud—I'd think, Maybe this is it. Maybe I'm ready to change. Maybe I'm finally changing.

But it was never about a single moment. It was the accumulation of almosts.

Moments that sparked hope but never stuck.
Moments that felt like turning points but turned into reruns.
Moments that whispered truth, but I wasn't ready to live it.

But the moment things got hard, I went right back to what I knew—comfort—knowing it would not work. That's what comfort does: it disguises itself as relief, but it was the trap that kept me stuck.

Because here's the truth: healing isn't comfortable. It's hard. It's not neat. It's not linear. Some days you feel like you're all over the place—other days, like you've arrived. Sometimes, healing even looks like failure.

When Change Finally Came

What finally started to change me wasn't a moment. It was exhaustion.

I kept doing the same things and expecting different results. I kept numbing the pain, only to find it waiting for me the next morning. I kept chasing a connection but still felt alone. I kept wanting to be seen but felt forgotten.

Eventually, I got tired of the cycle. Tired of pretending. Tired of hurting. Tired of waking up in the same place I swore I'd never return to.

But even then, there was still distance between being tired and truly surrendering.

Surrender is what finally opens the door to change.

Reflection Questions

- How is this emotional turmoil affecting your heart and your faith right now?
- Who is one person you can reach out to today for honest conversation or support?

⊃ Are you trying to escape your pain through distraction or silence? What's one small way you can start turning toward healing?

Practical Activity

Spend ten minutes journaling honestly about what your "new normal" feels like.

Write down three emotions or worries weighing heaviest on your heart.

Then choose one small step: a prayer, a phone call, scheduling a counseling session—and commit to doing it today.

Prayer

> Heavenly Father, I feel shaken—confused, hurt, and unsure of where You are in all of this. The weight feels heavy. The silence feels louder than ever. But I want to stop running. Draw near to me. Show me one step I can take today toward healing. I don't have it all figured out, but I'm still here—and I'm trusting You'll meet me in that. Amen.

CHAPTER 04
THE EMOTIONAL ANCHOR FINDING SAFE HARBOR IN THE STORM

Back in Chapter 1, I introduced the Big Four—the foundations I needed to rebuild: spiritual, emotional, physical, and financial health. At the time, I didn't know they were foundational. I just knew I was drowning.

This chapter marks the beginning of the first steps, particularly the emotional part. It wasn't born out of heroic clarity. It came from exhaustion. From that slow crawl forward after you've hit every wall. I was starting to realize I couldn't keep doing what I was doing—not because I had some grand insight—but because I was out of options.

We've all become so used to before-and-after stories that we forget how much life happens in between. This was that in-between space. Just some things I started doing to get through one more day. One more decision. One more moment of not falling apart. Nothing felt like transformation. It felt more like survival. But those steps mattered.

Something Had to Give

I was running on fumes.

The parties, the noise, the endless pretending, I called it living, but it was just another way to stay lost. I didn't feel like I was actively dying, but I sure wasn't living.

It felt like watching myself on a screen, a guy drifting alone in open water, grabbing at anything that might keep him afloat.

I was haunted by the fear that I would never be whole. Maybe I wasn't lovable. That this half-life—this shadow version of myself—was all I had left. And the worst part? A part of me started to believe it.

Still, the truth kept pushing its way in: none of it was working.

So I did the only thing I could think to do—I asked God for help.

I Didn't Know What I Was Doing (But I Started Anyway)

The strange thing is, I grew up in church. Christian high school. Christian college. I had all the verses memorized. I could check all the boxes. I was great at following the rules—until I wasn't.

At some point, I got tired of faking it. Tired of the hypocrisy. I had seen too many people act like they had it together while living completely different lives behind closed doors.

Of course, I was one of them.

I didn't want to admit that yet, but I knew.

Still, all those years of showing up to church—even when I wasn't really listening—something had seeped in. A verse. A sermon. A phrase I couldn't forget. It's like the words buried themselves somewhere deep and waited for the moment I might need them.

That moment had come.

You Have God's Ear

There was this one sermon that stuck with me, long before I ever knew I needed it.

The preacher was walking through the bold part, not the polite part. He slammed the pulpit and said, "ASK. Ask, ask, ask, ask, ask! Keep on asking! Keep on seeking! Keep on Knocking." It wasn't quiet. It wasn't gentle. It was a cry—a demand to go after God even when you feel like He's not answering.

And then he told the story from Luke 11:5-13 like this:

It's midnight. The house is dark. Kids are asleep. You're in bed, finally drifting off.

BAM. BAM. BAM.

A knock at the door.

You groan. Who the heck is knocking this late?

It's your buddy. He's desperate. A friend just showed up after a long trip, and he's got nothing to feed them. No bread. No snacks. Not even a cracker. He needs your help.

You yell through the door, "Man, it's late. I'm in bed. The kids are asleep. I'm not getting up."

But he doesn't stop.

He keeps knocking.

Not to be annoying. Not to manipulate. He needs help. And eventually—even if you don't get up because he's your friend—you'll get up to make it stop. You'll help him because he won't leave you alone.

That's the picture Jesus paints of prayer.

Not polished. Not perfect. Just persistent.

Keep knocking. Keep asking even if it feels awkward. Even if it feels too late, even if you feel like God should be asleep by now, he's not annoyed. He hears the knock.

When I finally took this seriously and prayed in this way for a few months, my entire life changed. Had I grasped this sooner, prayed like this sooner, imagine what God could have done. But the reality is, there are no plan Bs with the Lord.

It didn't become a pattern for me until there was nothing left but me and the Lord.

So, I used the prayer pattern outlined in Luke 11:1-4, not out of spiritual maturity but out of desperation. I needed something to ground me. And this rhythm became that anchor.

1. **Acknowledge God** – Start with who He is. Even when I didn't feel it, I'd speak it: God, You're still good. You're still here.

2. **Ask (and keep asking)** – That story in Luke about the neighbor knocking at midnight stuck with me. He keeps knocking until his neighbor gets up. That became me. I asked for peace. For direction. For mercy. For help to not do something stupid. I would quote God's word back to him. You said in Matthew 7:7-8 that we could "Ask and it will be given to you."

3. **Forgive and be forgiven** – I asked God to forgive me, knowing I didn't deserve it. And I started trying to forgive my ex, her family, and all the friends who disappeared after the divorce. It wasn't instant. But it was honest.

4. **Keep me out of trouble** – This was my daily request. Because I knew myself. I could spiral fast. Whether it was chasing women, chasing work, or chasing approval—I needed God to help me not wreck what little I had left.

Some days, I sat there in silence. Some days I rambled. Some days, I couldn't stop crying. But I showed up. And showing up became the win.

Moving My Body While My Heart Wasn't Onboard

My emotions were a mess. But I could move! That I could control.

After the partying and everything that came with it, I was out of shape—physically and emotionally. At first, the "divorce diet" kicked in. The weight dropped fast. But once the shock wore off and reality set in, I stopped caring. About my health. About my future. About myself.

It wasn't until a doctor's visit that everything hit. He looked me in the eye and said that if I didn't make changes, I might not be around long enough to watch my daughters grow up.

Then came the final gut punch: a photo from a fundraiser. I was holding a glass of wine, with a swollen face and red eyes. I barely recognized myself. That wasn't the man I wanted to be—especially not for my girls.

So, I started walking. Just around the block at first. Then jogging. Then the gym. Over time, the weight came off, back to what I weighed in college. But this wasn't about getting ripped. It was about staying alive.

I didn't have the strength to fix my heart yet. But I could move my body. And somehow, physical movement started to clear the mental fog.

Looking back now, I see this was one of the first signs I was starting to rebuild one of the Big Four—my physical health. Every walk, every workout, every drop of sweat was my body's way of saying, *I'm not done yet.*

Serving Without Making It About Me

I never thought serving others would be part of my healing. I thought I was too broken to be useful.

But I found myself helping at a local nonprofit—just moving boxes, setting up tables. Nothing glamorous. And I didn't go to talk about my pain. I went because I didn't want to be alone with it.

Something shifted in that space. I didn't feel transformed. But I did feel something I hadn't felt in a while—needed. Valued. Like, I still had something to offer.

And I learned quickly—this wasn't the place to unload my story. I watched other guys do it, and people quietly distanced themselves. I decided just to serve. And in doing that, I found room to breathe.

Learning Not to Do it Alone

Eventually, I knew I couldn't do it alone.

Initially, I ended up at a divorce group at a church I barely knew. I didn't want to be there, but I had nowhere else to go. I wasn't ready to talk. But I listened. And that was enough for a while.

Later, after hearing some of the guys talk about counseling, someone passed me a number. That's how I got connected with my counselor.

He wasn't a fixer. He didn't act like he had all the answers. But he listened. And over the next few years, he helped me sort through more than just the divorce.

We talked about childhood wounds. About my pornography addiction. My insecurities. My warped views of masculinity. We confronted the stuff I had buried long before the marriage began.

Counseling opened my eyes to the possibility of healing—and that maybe change wasn't impossible. It gave me space to be honest without being judged. And that alone was something I hadn't had before.

Reflect Through Journaling

I kept writing.

Some days I wrote one line. Other days, I filled page after page.

The journal became my mirror. A record of the mess, the progress, the moments I didn't want to forget—even when I was still living them.

Looking back now, those pages are proof that I kept going. That God kept showing up. That healing was happening—even if I couldn't always feel or see it.

I Was Still Living a Double Life

Here's the part I need to say plainly: I was doing all these things—praying, serving, counseling, journaling—and I was still bouncing back and forth between two lives.

One day, I was with church friends, praying and talking deeply about God. Next, I was out drinking with the guys. Next, I hooked up with a girl I was dating.

I was leading a double life.

And at church, I'd see guys just like me—smiling, saying the right things, but fighting the same battle. We were all hoping no one noticed.

What I've come to believe is that most people don't change until the pain of staying the same exceeds the pain of changing.

That line-in-the-sand moment? That realization came much later, after a financial storm and through rejection.

But here—right here—is when I started to feel the fatigue.

And sometimes, getting tired is the first sign of awakening.

You Don't Need a Plan—just a Step (Psalm 37:23).

So maybe that's where you are right now.

Not ready for radical change. Not ready for dramatic confessions.

Just tired.

That's okay.

You don't need a perfect strategy. You need one real step.

A walk.
A prayer.
A journal entry.
A conversation.

Many gurus online sell their plans, but most of us never get past the first step. We get stuck because we look too far ahead. That's how I used to get sidetracked. I'd think about everything that needed to change in me—every failure, every broken piece—and sure enough, I'd shut down and go back to comfort.

It's why God said, "Don't worry about tomorrow…"

Because sometimes, we lose today at the cost of a tomorrow that never comes.

So don't overthink it.

Start small. Start honestly. Start here.

Reflection Questions

- What's one small step you can take this week that would feel like progress—even if it's scary?
- Are you clinging to any comforts that might be keeping you stuck?
- Who could you reach out to—honestly—for support, not solutions?

Practical Activity

Write a one-sentence journal entry tonight. Just one. Even if it's: "God, I don't know where to begin."
Then go for a short walk—alone, without distractions. Let it be what it is. A beginning.

Prayer

> God, I don't feel strong. I don't even feel ready. But I'm tired of doing what doesn't work. Tired of pretending. Tired of numbing. So I'm here. And I'm asking—please meet me in this. Help me take the next step, whatever that looks like. Surround me with the right people. Protect me from going backward. And remind me—daily—that I am not alone. Amen.

CHAPTER 05
THE STAGES OF DIVORCE RECOVERY

The divorce fallout didn't come with a warning. There were no signs saying, "You're entering stage one" or "This will pass in six months." It just hit—wave after wave—like standing in the ocean with no clue when the next breaker was coming. Some knocked me over. Some numbed me. And some I didn't even see until years later.

I didn't know there were "stages" of grief. I just thought I was losing my mind. But over time, I began to see patterns. I started naming what I was walking through—not to label it, but to survive it. Naming gave shape to the chaos.

The stages didn't arrive in order. They overlapped. Looped. Returned when I thought I was past them. But each one brought something important, even when it just brought the realization that I wasn't okay.

These aren't steps to follow. They're not a timeline. They're just the messy, sacred, human process of walking through grief—and finding your footing again.

This is what it looked like for me.

Denial

It showed up first, not with a bang, but like fog that wouldn't lift. At first, I kept thinking, *"This can't be real,"* and I'd wake up one morning to find everything back to normal. That something or someone—God, a pastor, a friend—would step in and press rewind. We were Christians. We had kids. We weren't that couple.

But we were. And it was real.

Looking back, the shock and awe of that first night was just the beginning. Denial was the soundtrack that followed—quiet, persistent, convincing me that maybe this could still all go away. Maybe I just misunderstood something. Maybe if I prayed hard enough, or said the right words, or waited long enough, she'd change her mind.

There's a strange kindness in denial. It's like the body's way of cushioning the fall. But if you stay there too long, it becomes quicksand. I found myself stuck in stillness. Sitting on the edge of my bed, staring at the wall, hoping time would reverse.

I went to church. I smiled. I told people I was "doing okay." Then I'd go home and cry in the bathroom with the water running so my girls wouldn't hear. I wasn't ready to face it yet. I didn't want to tell the truth out loud, because that would make it real.

But as the days dragged on, reality crept in. I couldn't pretend forever. When denial finally began to fade, I was left staring at what I didn't want to face.

The more I accepted what had happened, the more desperate I became too un-happen it. I replayed conversations, rewrote endings in my head, and tried to bargain my way back to a life that was already gone.

Bargaining

This is the stage no one likes to admit. This is where I started trying to make deals with God.

> "If you'll just restore this marriage, I'll do anything. I'll serve more. I'll change. Just please... fix it."

I thought if I could carry enough guilt or show enough repentance, maybe she'd see something different. I wrote long letters, had emotional conversations, tried to reach her through her dad, through friends, through anything.

One letter I wrote said:

"I believe God joined us. I believe it was His will. And the thought of us being apart has broken me to pieces."

I wasn't just owning my part—I was trying to own it all. Bargaining led me to believe that if I could feel bad enough, I might be able to fix it.

Looking back, I realized what I was doing. I wasn't surrendering to God. I was trying to control Him, trying to bargain my way out of pain, trying to write a script where I could be the hero who rescued the story.

But that's not how grace works. And it's not how healing works either.

Real healing doesn't come from rescue fantasies. It comes from surrender.

And when those efforts didn't work, bargaining gave way to something far heavier.

Anger

I didn't just visit anger. I rented space there. Put up curtains. Hung a welcome sign.

There were moments I didn't even recognize myself. My journal is filled with phrases like "I'll show her" and "She destroyed everything." Every interaction—every legal form, every text—felt like gasoline on a fire I didn't know how to put out.

I filtered the world through pain. Every sermon, every well-meaning friend, even my kids, everything became a reminder of what was lost.

But here's the thing about anger: underneath it, there's always grief. My rage wasn't just about her. It was about me. About what I'd lost. About what I feared I'd never have again.

Anger made me feel powerful, like I wasn't a victim. But it was a false strength. The longer I held onto it, the more it held onto me.

What softened wasn't the pain—it was my perspective. I realized I wasn't standing outside the wreckage—I'd helped build it. And facing that truth was the beginning of freedom. That's when grace started to show up. Not soft grace. Not churchy grace. Real grace.

The kind that lets you hurt but doesn't let the hurt define you.

And with grace came something I hadn't felt in a while—hope, not for reconciliation. Just for a future I couldn't see yet.

But hope doesn't erase the crash that came afterward.

When the anger finally drained out of me, it didn't leave peace behind. It left a vacuum—and that vacuum filled with something darker.

Depression

This wasn't just sadness. This was a darkness that got into my bones.

I stopped eating. Dropped from 210 to 155. Couldn't sleep. Couldn't think. I'd sit in a room for hours, doing nothing, just staring, just existing. Everything felt heavy—every breath an effort.

Some of my journal entries from that time still shake me:

"If I died right now, no one would find me for days."
"Breakdown time…"
"All I thought was real was a lie."

This was the bottom. Or at least, it felt like it.

But somehow, even there, I wasn't alone. I started talking to someone. A counselor. A group. A friend. And even though nothing changed right away, I wasn't drowning alone anymore.

That was the beginning of a different kind of strength.

Acceptance

People throw this word around like it means everything's fine. It doesn't.

Acceptance is quiet. It's subtle. It's not a celebration, it's a breath. A slow, deep breath where your body finally stops fighting reality.

For me, it came slowly, over months, years. It came in routines. In the shift from asking "why?" to asking "what now?"

One journal entry captured it best:

"Acceptance of my lot in life is easy, but the feelings of the old are hard to break."

Exactly. You can know the facts and still feel the ache.

But acceptance isn't the end—it's the beginning. It's the place where healing starts to catch up with you, where you begin to hope without needing everything to make sense first.

It's when you start building again—not to replace what was lost, but to rebuild from what remains.

Spiritual Awakening

This stage didn't come easy for me. It came alongside acceptance. When the bargaining faded, and the anger burned out, when I'd survived depression and stopped pretending—it was then that something deeper started stirring.

I didn't have a mountaintop moment. I didn't hear God's voice in a lightning bolt.

But slowly, I began to wonder: *Is God still here?*

I'd show up at church hungover from the night before, hoping something would stick. I'd be zealous one week, then go right back to the same destructive patterns the next.

But even then—even in my inconsistency—I began to see glimmers of grace.

It started with a line in my journal:

"God, You know my heart. Forgive me. Convict me. Change me."

I didn't feel holy when I wrote that. I felt desperate. But desperation has a way of unlocking surrender.

I had to fight to believe that God still wanted me. That I wasn't disqualified. That I hadn't messed it all up beyond repair.

But the more I opened that door, the more I found Him waiting.

You're Not Crazy. You're Grieving.

So if you're cycling through these stages—if some of them feel like old friends and others feel brand new—let me say this:

You're not crazy. You're grieving.

This isn't about checking boxes.

Some of these stages stay longer than others. Anger and depression wore out their welcome in my story. Bargaining came early and left fast. Spiritual awakening rose up slowly, tied tightly to acceptance. But they all played a part.

You may not know where you are right now. That's okay.

But you're not stuck forever. There is life after this.

Reflection Questions

- Which stage are you living in right now—or bouncing between?
- What's been helping you move through it (or keeping you stuck)?
- Is there a thread of hope you can hold onto today?

Practical Activity

Write down one phrase you keep telling yourself in this season, especially one rooted in pain or fear.

Then, underneath it, write a second line that starts with: *But God...*

Example:
"I'll never feel whole again."
But God restores the brokenhearted.

Keep it where you'll see it. Let truth speak back to fear.

Prayer

God, You see the mess. The numbness. The anger. The tears I don't let anyone else see. I want to believe there's something on the other side of this. But I don't always feel it. I don't even always believe it. Still—I'm here. Teach me how to breathe again. Help me stop pretending. Show me that grace still applies to me. And give me the courage to take one more step. In Jesus' name, Amen.

CHAPTER 06
A YEAR OF HEALING MY DIVORCE JOURNEY

The first year wasn't a comeback. It was a collection of messy, barely holding-on moments that eventually added up to progress.

And the only place I could make sense of it was on paper.

Journaling became the one place I could be completely honest—when I couldn't talk to God, or my friends, or even myself, without filtering. The page never judged me. It just held what I couldn't carry out loud.

So, what follows isn't a clean reflection or a well-told story. It's the middle—the fog. The part of the journey where nothing feels finished and everything still hurts. But it's also the part where something begins to shift—where I start to see God not in the outcome, but in the process.

Excerpts from My Journal

Day 31 – Stunned

Last month, my wife told me she wanted a divorce, and it struck like a storm I didn't see coming. I'm not one for big emotions, yet I can't eat or sleep—feeling is all I've got left. Time drags in slow motion, and I'm adrift, unmoored from everything I knew.

Day 32 – The Papers

Picking up the divorce papers today broke me in ways I wasn't ready for. Screaming, crying, cursing—things I never thought I'd let out—overwhelmed me. Seeing our marriage boiled down to legal pages feels like the end of it all.

Day 37 – Finding Small Hope

Each day, I search for hope in little things—a kind word, a task done. Slowing my thoughts eases the flood of emotions. Wanting to heal feels like the first step toward being whole again.

Day 40 – Endless Questions

Work feels unbearable—my mind's lost in endless questions: Is this my fault? Will I ever feel whole? Loneliness amplifies every doubt, and I'm struggling to release what I thought was true.

Day 46 – Watching the Void

Tonight, I watched a movie alone in this empty house. It's strange living where every corner holds a memory of someone, now a stranger. Loneliness and dread of what's next weigh heavily.

Day 51 – Anger and Frustration

A gray day of small errands and forced small talk. Washing the car brought a fleeting sense of normalcy. Anger bubbles beneath, stirred by well-meaning but draining advice from others.

Day 64 – Slim Hopes

Every time my children leave, adjusting to their absence cuts deep. I cling to a faint hope she might turn back, though I know it's unlikely. My mind sees it's over, but my heart won't let go.

Day 66 – Balancing Decisions

I'm wrestling with renting or buying a home—a choice heavy with emotion. Buying feels like hope and stability; renting feels fleeting and insufficient. I'm praying for clarity in this uncharted place.

Day 67 – Anger and Fear

Learning she dropped me from her health insurance without warning left me furious and afraid. Every exchange with her feels like a fight, and I'm overwhelmed by uncertainty over where I'll land. This pushes me to lean on God for strength.

Day 68 – An Empty Home

The house sold fast, and now I face finding a new place. Its emptiness mirrors the void within me. Amid fear and frustration, I'm learning to trust God's provision.

Day 70 – Decisions Weigh Heavy

Running errands and packing for the move feels unreal. Memories of childhood homelessness rise up, heightening my fear of choosing wrong. Yet I remind myself faith means trusting God when the future's unclear.

Day 72 – A New Beginning

I chose to buy a smaller house that feels manageable. This marks a step toward reclaiming my life and finding hope. The financial strain is real, but the thought of my own space brings peace.

Day 78 – Bittersweet Moments

A weekend with my children lifted me, yet it underscored what's lost. Each moment with them drives home the end of our marriage. Church today offered hope, teaching me to rest in God's promises.

Day 83 – Lonely but Thankful

A quiet Friday night—loneliness a familiar guest. Reflecting on God's faithfulness reminds me I'm never truly alone. Songs like Jeremy Camp's "I Still Believe" help keep hope alive.

Day 85 – The Move

Movers came today, leaving the house hollow, echoing with memories. I wept briefly, then embraced the chance to start fresh. Despite the ache, I feel God is guiding me through this shift.

Day 87 – Conflict and Closure

A tense talk with her laid bare the hurt on both sides. I spoke of my love one last time, though she brushed it off. These moments drive me to pray for peace and strength to move on.

Day 92 – New Strength

Life's a cycle of work, prayer, and seeking God's peace. My divorce group has been a steady source of strength and perspective. Letting go of bitterness is tough, but I trust God to heal my heart.

Day 101 – A New Home

Moved into my new house today—an emotional day of sadness and hope. Each room's a blank slate, a chance to rebuild. God's blessings shine even in the hardest times.

Day 102 – Writing for Peace

I've wrestled with writing her a letter to voice my heart and find closure. My group urged me to release it constructively. This shows me how far I've come and how God's carried me.

Day 111 – A Final Letter

Wrote her one last letter, knowing it wouldn't sway her but seeking my peace. I wanted my girls to see, and I tried to leave nothing unsaid. Writing eased the lingering pain and opened the door to hope for what's ahead.

Day 115 – Grieving Dreams

Time with my children stirs dreams I held for our family—growing old together, lasting love. Their loss overwhelms me. Yet I'm resolved to grieve them, trusting God to redeem what's next.

Day 121 – Friendship Restored

An old friend, also divorced, brought light to this dark stretch. Laughter, talk, and shared understanding made me feel alive again. New friendships ease loneliness, showing the value of connection.

Day 141 – A Release of Tears

Back from an 8-day trip, I walked in and broke down unexpectedly. This home, free of her memories, still became a safe place for buried grief to rise. It reminds me healing's slow, needing time and grace.

Day 158 – Losing Everyone

Hearing a mutual friend call me "the bad one" stung deep. The divorce took not just my marriage but the ties I cherished with them. I hold that God sees the truth—His view of me matters most.

Day 170 – New Challenges

Her legal moves feel like attacks, draining me emotionally and financially. Anger tempts me, but I cling to God's promise of wisdom and peace. This trial teaches me to trust His plan, even when it's heavy.

Day 181 – Reflecting on Loss

As the settlement nears, emotions flood—looking through old photos brought sorrow and gratitude for what was. The pain's fresh, but I trust healing will come with time.

Day 196 – The Weight of It All

Scanning marriage photos is painful yet freeing—each one a reminder of what I had, what I lost. It's hard, but it's part of accepting the past and moving toward a brighter tomorrow.

Day 204 – Signing the Papers

Signing the papers was one of my hardest days—dropping them at her lawyer's felt like sealing our marriage's end. Heartbroken, I trust God will carry me forward.

Day 228 – The Battle of the Mind

Grieving this loss feels like a relentless fight in my mind—some days hopeful, others dark and empty. I take it one day at a time, trusting this pain is a fleeting part of a greater plan.

Day 269 – Letting Go of the Past

I've learned moving forward means not dwelling on what's gone. Focusing on now and what's ahead helps me rediscover who I am. Letting go's tough, but it's the path to true healing.

Day 275 – Choosing to Live

Watching a friend's divorce finalize stirred my own memories—God's faithfulness carried me through, and I've come far. I choose to live well, not just endure, and to lift others to find joy in their pain.

Day 301 – The Framework of Love

A sermon on 1 Corinthians 13 showed how far I'd strayed from true love in my marriage—patient, kind, selfless traits I often lacked. Moving on, I aim to live these in all my ties.

Day 334 – Facing the Past

A trip to where I proposed brought a sudden wave of grief—memories of happier days, her birthday, and our anniversary this month weighed heavily. The pain's sharp, but I hold hope for what's coming.

Day 365 – A Year Later

Hard to believe it's been a year since this began. The pain lingers, but I'm grateful for God's faithfulness in bringing me this far. It's a testament to resilience, healing, and hope that life will get better.

Drawing Strength from the Year

Reading those journal entries now, I see it more clearly—this wasn't a year of fixing things. It was a year of finding God amid the wreckage.

He didn't rush me. He didn't shame me. He walked with me, slowly, faithfully, while I stumbled forward.

Some days I still read those pages—not to dwell in the pain, but to remember that even my messiest moments were not wasted. They were part of the becoming who God created me to be.

Not all storms bring closure. But they do uncover what's unshakable. And that year, through grief, through survival, through flickers of hope—I began to believe that maybe God wasn't finished with me yet.

Stepping Forward with Resilience

The year also didn't give me all the answers. But it gave me endurance. It revealed who I was when everything was stripped away—and who I was becoming when I chose to keep showing up.

I wasn't the same man who signed those papers. But I also wasn't healed—not even close. That year didn't fix me; it just kept me moving. Each step forward was clumsy, uneven, and often followed by a few steps back. But I was learning how to walk again—slowly, painfully, honestly.

Psalm 37:23-24 became a reminder:

> 23
> *The steps of a man are established by the Lord,*
> *when he delights in his way;*

24
though he fall, he shall not be cast headlong,
for the Lord upholds his hand.

That was me—falling, rising, falling again.

Reflection Questions

- What moment in your first year struck you deepest, and how did you find your way through it?
- Where has God shown up in your chaos, and what small victory can you note today?
- What's one step you can take this week to release the past, piece by piece?

Practical Activity

Take your journal—write one entry this week, as raw as it comes. Pick a day that stands out, pour it out, then note one way God's held you through it. Let it rest; see what stirs in your heart.

Prayer

> Heavenly Father, Thank You for staying with me through this year of struggle and hope, lifting me when I couldn't rise on my own. Show me Your hand in the chaos, help me release what's past, and guide me to trust You with what's ahead. Heal me slowly and surely until I stand firmer in You. In Jesus' name, Amen.

CHAPTER 07
WALKING THROUGH LONELINESS WITH STRENGTH

The first year had passed. I'd moved into my new house. I'd survived the legal chaos. I'd stopped wondering if she would come back. And while a part of me expected the weight to lift after all that, a different kind of heaviness settled in.

I had made it through the storm, but now came the silence.

There were no more papers to sign. No big fights. Just... quiet.

It was the first time I wasn't busy reacting. And that's when loneliness came in—not as a wave, but as a slow, creeping tide. The noise had faded, but the ache had only grown deeper.

I didn't know how to live in this stillness.

At first, I filled it with motion. I said yes to everything. Stayed out late. Ran errands that didn't need to be run. I worked too much, scrolled too long, dated too soon. I would drive 30 minutes out of the way just to eat in a busy diner because I didn't want to go home.

I wasn't trying to rebuild my life—I was trying to outrun the empty parts of it.

That's what loneliness does. It doesn't always announce itself with tears. Sometimes, it looks like being constantly occupied. I told myself I was strong, that I was healing. But really, I was avoiding. I could be surrounded by people and still feel miles from connection.

And when the noise faded—when the girls went back to their mom's, when the weekend plans fell through, when the phone stayed quiet—I'd feel the full weight of it again.

Loneliness doesn't always scream. Sometimes it settles in empty spaces.

The Ache Beneath the Surface

I thought I missed her. And in some ways, I did. But as time passed, I realized what I missed most wasn't her—it was the familiarity of being known. Of having someone to share the little things with. Of sitting in silence with another person and not needing to explain yourself.

I missed that version of me. The one who used to feel steady in a room, who didn't constantly question if he still mattered.

And it wasn't just emotional. It was physical too. The untouched side of the bed. The empty seat at the table. The sound of my own voice being the only one in the house. All of it reminded me of what was gone.

But more than anything, it reminded me that I didn't know who I was without her.

That's what loneliness strips away—your reflections. Without someone else's gaze, you're forced to face your own. And for a long time, I didn't like what I saw.

Learning to Sit in It

I remember one night, sitting in the living room—TV off, phone dead, lights dim. The girls had just left after the weekend, and I sat there for hours—not crying, not praying, just breathing and listening to the silence. Feeling it settle around me like a heavy blanket.

Five Keys That Helped Me Face Loneliness

I'm not giving you a formula here. They're just pieces of the road I walked—things that helped me move forward when the weight of being alone felt like too much.

1. **Changing Perspective**

    One cold morning, I was driving into town under thick, gray skies. The kind that presses down on your chest. But when I turned north onto the highway, something changed. The clouds broke. Light poured through. I hadn't changed anything but my direction.

    That moment stuck with me. It reminded me how small shifts can alter our perspective. I started saying Psalm 34:18 out loud in the car—not because I felt it, but because I needed to hear it. *The Lord is close to the brokenhearted.* And slowly, I began to believe it. Not every day. But some days.

    I needed three things to make this shift in perspective: *a readiness to see it anew, a resolve to look beyond the hurt, and a trust that He's near.* Some men I've met in my divorce group found shelter in that truth right after their splits, resting in Him through the fog. For me, this turning began slowly. When I started affirming that He was still with me, it helped me shift from despair to something more honest and hopeful.

2. **Breaking Isolation**

    I used to avoid being home alone, so I stayed busy. Surrounded myself with noise. I'd go to diners in the morning, coffee shops at night, anywhere I could be near others without really being with them. The presence of people gave me the illusion of connection, but the emptiness remained when I got home.

One night, I decided to turn on some music I heard at church. I played it and just sat. No talking. No agenda. Just sitting. It didn't cure the ache, but it created space for God to speak into it.

That space became a lifeline. Some nights I read Scripture. Some nights, I sat in silence. But I kept showing up. And slowly, the presence of God became real to me again—not in a religious way, but in a relational one. Romans 8:39 reminded me that nothing separates us from His love. Psalm 139 says His thoughts about me outnumber the grains of sand. And somehow, in those moments, I began to believe them. Not because I felt different, but because I trusted that He was still writing my comeback, even in the silence.

3. **Shifting from Complaints to Gratitude**

    There was a season when my prayers sounded like rants. I'd pour out every frustration, disappointment, and fear—and honestly, it felt good at first. But after a while, it started to poison my own heart. I'd finish praying and feel more bitter than before.

    That's when I started noticing the pattern. I was rehearsing the hurt, not releasing it.

    David had a different pattern for his complaints in Psalm 142. He poured out his complaint—but then he shifted. He said, *When my spirit grows faint within me, it is You who watch over my way.*

    That's what I started trying to do. I'd begin angry or numb or hurt—but I wouldn't stop there. I'd finish by speaking truth back to myself: You see me. You haven't left me. You are still good.

    Over time, I also began learning when to share with others. Not everyone could hold my pain well. But my friend Jason could. He never fixed me—he just listened. Gave me space. Let me vent, then gently reminded me what was true. That's what I needed. Not a solution—just presence.

Gratitude didn't come naturally. It came with time.

4. **Choosing Praise and Thankfulness**

    The day I got the divorce papers, I shattered. I journaled in all caps: SCREAMING. CRYING. HEARTBREAKING. I had nothing but pain. But sixty days later, I flipped back through that same journal and found a new entry: "These lonely times draw me to God. So renewing. So thankful."

    I don't remember writing that. But it reminded me that healing was already happening—even when I didn't feel it.

    So I started thanking God for things I didn't understand: Thank You for this pain. Use it. Thank you for this quiet—meet me in it. It felt strange at first. But over time, it became a new pattern. Praise grounded me when everything else felt unstable.

5. **Make Peace with Loneliness**

    I used to think peace meant the ache would go away. That one day I'd wake up and feel whole again. But now I know peace is learning to live well, even with the ache.

    A guy at church used to say, "Let go and let God." I didn't love the phrase back then. It felt like a cop-out. But now, I get it. Sometimes, you're holding so tightly to what was—or what you thought would be—that you miss what is.

    There's a line in Psalm 37 that says God orders our steps—but it doesn't say He explains them. I've learned to stop demanding clarity and start asking for presence.

Stepping Forward with Strength

Loneliness still visits. I won't lie. But it doesn't own me anymore. It's part of my story—but it's not the end.

Over the years, I've found new rhythms. I've built friendships. I've laughed again. I've dated again—and eventually, I found love again. But even then, I learned that only God can fill the emptiness that loneliness leaves behind.

That's what He does. He doesn't erase our emptiness—He enters it. He shapes us in it. He doesn't rush us out of the pain; He walks with us through it.

Reflection Questions

- Which part of your loneliness feels the heaviest right now, and have you invited God into it?
- Which of the five keys above have you tried before? Which might be worth trying now?
- Who in your life offers presence without pressure? Can you reach out to them this week?

Practical Activity

Pick one of the five keys. Write down what it might look like for you this week. Then commit to trying it once. Not forever. Just once. Then reflect on how it felt—honestly. That's enough.

Prayer

> Heavenly Father, You see the ache I can't always name. You know the loneliness I try to hide. Meet me in it. Not with noise or distraction, but with presence. Remind me that

> You're near. Help me make peace with the quiet. And show me that being alone doesn't mean being unloved. Walk with me, even here. Amen.

CHAPTER 08
RECLAIMING YOUR IDENTITY AFTER DIVORCE

When everything ended, I didn't just lose her—I lost the man I thought I was. The titles I once carried, husband, partner, protector—didn't fade gently. They were torn away, taking pieces of me with them.

I didn't see it at first. I thought I was navigating the fallout, trying to find my footing again. But underneath the surface, something deeper was happening; I was losing myself.

I still had roles—father, business owner, friend—but the one that had quietly anchored me, husband, was gone. And with it, the comfort of knowing who I was in the world. I remember looking in the mirror one morning and not recognizing the man staring back. I looked the same, but something essential had shifted.

That shift was slow. Subtle. Identity doesn't collapse like a house in a storm—it erodes, like a shoreline being pulled out to sea.

The Weight of Lost Identity

I didn't walk around saying, "Who am I now?" But that question was always humming in the background.

I felt it at church, surrounded by married couples, slipping into the back row like I didn't belong. I felt it when I dropped the kids off and returned to a quiet house, unsure of what to do with myself. I felt it in conversations where I found myself exaggerating things just to sound okay.

There was something about my dad growing up that never sat right with me. He had a way of stretching the truth—making things sound better than they were. As a kid, I'd feel this quiet embarrassment because I knew the real story. I told myself I'd never do that.

For most of my life, I didn't. I was honest—almost to a fault. But after the divorce, I caught myself doing the very thing I used to criticize. Telling stories that made me look more successful than I was. Acting like I was fine when I was crumbling.

I wasn't trying to deceive. I was trying to survive. To hold onto some version of "the man" I thought I needed to be. I didn't want to admit I felt small. Or lost. Or unsure of my worth without her.

And it wasn't just with words—I started projecting an image. Stretching myself financially to look like I had things together. The car. The boat. The watch. Hosting dinners. Picking up tabs. Building a reputation. Before long, I was getting awards. Featured in the press. Hanging with all the important people. I was working hard to become someone. But deep down, I felt empty—because I knew I was spinning something that didn't match the man inside.

I remember standing on stage receiving one of those awards. Friends clapped. Smiles all around. But inside, I felt nothing. It was all for show. That identity, the one built to impress, was built on sand.

What Divorce Tried to Name Me

Shame is sneaky. It doesn't shout—it creeps. It wraps itself in phrases like "You're not enough" or "You blew it." I'd feel it in glances at church or in the unspoken silence when friends didn't know what to say. Most of the time, it wasn't even about what others thought; it was about what I believed about myself.

In the divorce group, I remember one guy saying, "I feel like a nobody now." I knew exactly what he meant. When a role you've held for years disappears, it messes with your sense of worth. I wasn't her husband anymore. And for a while, I wasn't sure who I was at all.

But there was a whisper—quieter, steadier—the kind that doesn't come from within, but from above. It came through Scripture, through prayer, through friends who reminded me of who I was, even when I forgot.

Verses like Genesis 1:27, "So God created man in His own image," began to take on a different meaning. Not as churchy affirmations, but as anchors. Reminders that my identity didn't start with marriage, and it wouldn't end with divorce. That I was crafted by God, not labeled by failure.

My friend Jason helped me see it, too. He never let me spiral too far before asking, "What's God's truth in this?" And over time, I started to answer that question myself.

Becoming Again

Ephesians 2:10 became a lifeline: "For we are God's handiwork, created in Christ Jesus to do good works, which God prepared in advance for us to do." That verse told me my life still had purpose. That I wasn't on the bench. I wasn't discarded. I was still in the game, even if I didn't feel like it.

However, reclaiming that identity wasn't a single big breakthrough—it was a series of small moments. A decision to show up with God. A quiet night reading Scripture instead of numbing out. A conversation with a friend where I told the truth instead of pretending.

Here's what it looked like for me:

- **Speaking Truth Aloud** – Some mornings, I'd stand in front of the mirror and say, "I'm God's handiwork." Not because

I believed it—but because I needed to hear it. Over time, it started to stick.

- **Leaning on Safe Voices** – Jason was one of those for me. He didn't let me forget who I was, even when I wanted to. I had to learn to let others speak into my life when I didn't trust my own voice.

- **Serving in Small Ways** – I started helping at church again. Nothing big—just simple things. But even small acts reminded me that I still had something to give. That God wasn't done with me and I needed community.

- **Journaling the Real Stuff** – Not polished prayers—just raw thoughts. I'd write what I was feeling and then try to answer it with truth. Not always neatly. But honestly.

- **Sitting in His Presence** – I'd read Psalm 139:14—"I am fearfully and wonderfully made"—and let it linger. Some nights, I didn't even read. I just sat. Letting God see me. Letting Him name me again.

It Wasn't Instant, But It Was Real

I didn't check boxes, and suddenly feel whole again. I still wrestled, still doubted, still had days where I questioned everything.

I wish I could say this season marked the full return of my identity—but it didn't. It was just one piece of a larger story. The unraveling had slowed, and something truer was beginning to take shape. But I hadn't yet let go of all the ego—not the pride, not the part of me that still needed to be seen, admired, validated. That surrender would come later—after the financial collapse, rejection, and the moment I finally drew a line in the sand and gave it all to God.

Even now, I still keep an eye on it—the spin, the drive to perform. I see it for what it is. But these days, I use that same energy to help, not to hide. That's what grace does. It repurposes what once broke you into something that blesses others.

And looking back, I can see something real was taking shape, a quiet shift inside me. I had started listening again, not to shame or validation, but to the quiet voice that had been there all along.

Reflection Questions

- What lies about your identity have felt the loudest since the divorce?
- Which moment from this chapter echoes something you've felt?
- What small practice—truth-telling, journaling, serving—might help you reclaim who you are?

Practical Activity

Take 10 minutes this week. Write down one thing you've believed about yourself since the divorce that's not true. Then write down a verse or truth that speaks something better. Sit with it. Let it be a seed.

Prayer

> God, I've let my mistakes and losses shape how I see myself. But You say I'm Yours. Crafted. Loved. Seen. Help me believe that again. Help me live from that place. Speak louder than the shame. In Jesus' name, Amen.

CHAPTER 09
LETTING GOD DEFEND YOUR NAME

When the marriage ended, the hardest part wasn't the silence at home; it was the silence from people who once knew me. I didn't just lose a wife; I lost the benefit of the doubt. The quiet assumption that I was a good man was gone. It felt like everyone had a version of my story—and none of them came from me.

At church, the looks weren't cruel, just... cautious as if I were radioactive. A guy from my divorce group once said, "My old friends won't even talk to me. Like I'm contagious." I knew exactly what he meant. I told myself it didn't matter.

But it did.

I didn't want to be known as *the divorced guy*. I didn't want to be talked about. I just wanted to be known for who I really was. But I wasn't even sure who that was anymore—and I definitely wasn't in control of what people believed.

That's when the ache really set in.

The Weight of Being Misunderstood

This picked up right where Identity left off. In Chapter 8, I was unraveling on the inside. But this was external—watching the world draw its own conclusions while I couldn't explain my truth.

The stories flew fast. Mutual friends drifted. People picked sides. People filled in blanks with guesses or gossip. And every time I tried to explain or correct, it only made things worse.

I remember sitting in the car after a conversation where someone had repeated something they "heard." I was fuming. Not at them—but at the fact that truth didn't seem to matter.

I wanted to yell, "That's not true. That's not how it happened." But I didn't. I'd tried that before. It backfired. Either it stirred up more drama, or it made me look petty.

So, I stopped talking. At first, the silence felt forced, but over time it became familiar.

It wasn't fair, but it was where I found myself—learning to live with what I couldn't control.

The Shift That Helped Me Breathe Again

One day, while journaling, I wrote: "God sees the truth. Sooner or later, He will win." That gave me hope that whatever came my way, God knew—and His truth would stand.

But if I'm honest, there were days I didn't think His truth would win. I wanted the story corrected, the air cleared, for someone to say, "We were wrong about you."

All that did was keep the wound open.

So, whenever the noise grew louder than my strength, I'd pray, "Sooner or later, You will win, God."

And something began to shift. Not the talk. Not the rumors.

Me.

When I finally stopped trying to manage my reputation and let God carry it, I could breathe again.

Psalm 25:3 became an anchor: "No one who hopes in You will ever be put to shame."

The truth hadn't disappeared—it was being written in a quieter place.

And that's where grace began to rewrite the story.

When Grace Takes Over

For a long time, I thought defending myself meant walking out when I wasn't welcome. I thought setting boundaries meant burning bridges.

But I've learned grace looks different. Sometimes it stays. Not because others earned it—but because God is still working.

I saw that play out in a church group I joined, led by a young woman named Denise and overseen by a married couple, Jared and Laura.

One Sunday, I overheard Jared whisper to Denise, "Stay clear of him—he's divorced."

It cut deep. Not just because it was unfair—but because I wanted to shout, You don't know me… But I didn't. I stayed. Week after week. Made friends. Stayed present. Learned more about God.

Years later, Denise married James—a divorced man—and they built a beautiful life. James became an early reader of this book and offered some of the most thoughtful feedback I received. At their wedding reception, Jared pulled me aside and apologized. I smiled and said, "It's okay—it'll end up in the book somewhere," and we laughed.

Through that group, I found some of the best friendships of my life. Jared is now a friend and brother in Christ. And through Denise's sister, I met Kara—my wife—years after that first painful interaction.

If I had walked away? If I'd burned that bridge? I might have missed all of it.

Living Above the Noise

I won't pretend I never cared again. I did. Sometimes, I still do.

There are days when old wounds get reopened, when whispers sting. But I've learned how to breathe through it.

Here's what helped:

- **Guarding my thoughts.** When the lies came—*You're the failure. She was right to leave*—I paused. Let God speak louder.
- **Avoiding the bait.** Gossip. Bitterness. Retaliation. None of it healed me. "I'd rather not talk about her" became a lifeline.
- **Letting God speak for me.** That was the hardest. Trusting that over time, the truth would rise, and it did. God did win!

Some people came back. Others didn't. But I kept showing up. With God. For my kids. For the life I still had. That was enough.

Romans 8:31 stayed taped to my mirror: *"If God is for us, who can be against us?"*

It wasn't about defiance. It was about remembering who mattered most.

Let Him Carry What You Can't

You don't have to win the argument. You don't have to make everyone understand.

That's not your job.

Your job is to live with integrity—to stay steady, to keep becoming the man God sees, even when no one else does.

That kind of restraint takes strength. Real strength.

Letting God defend my name gave me something far more valuable than validation.

It gave me peace.

And over time, I began to believe that who I am isn't tied to what people say, or what was lost, or what I failed to explain.

It's tied to the One who already knows—and still calls me His.

Reflection Questions

- What judgment or rumor has stayed with you the longest?
- Where are you still trying to defend yourself instead of surrendering it to God?
- What would it look like to release one piece of that weight today?

Practical Activity

Write down one situation where you've been misunderstood or unfairly labeled. Pray over it. Then write underneath:

"God, I give this to You. You know the truth. You know me."

Tear it up. Or burn it. Or fold it and put it in your Bible. Whatever helps you release it.

Prayer

God, You see the truth even when no one else does. You know the full story. Help me stop fighting battles You've already won. Give me strength to stay silent when silence is holy. Help me release what I can't control. You hold my name. You hold my story. You hold my future. And that's enough. In Jesus' name, Amen.

CHAPTER 10
FORGIVENESS THE HARDEST, MOST IMPORTANT STEP

Letting go of how others saw me gave me space to breathe again. But the real work of healing began when I had to face something harder: forgiveness.

At first, it felt impossible. I wore anger like armor. I told myself bitterness was justified, proof that I'd been wronged. That she left. That she gave up. That I was the one fighting for our family.

And for a while, that narrative worked. It made me feel righteous. Wounded. Safe.

But underneath all that... I knew better.

We'd both made choices that fractured what we built. She didn't carry all the blame. And I wasn't innocent, not even close.

That realization crept in through quiet moments. A sermon. A journal entry. A quiet truth from a friend. The slow, unwanted truth: *I had hurt her, too.* I'd failed her in ways I didn't want to admit—emotionally, spiritually, and physically. I knew it. And I couldn't pretend forever.

Bitterness wasn't protecting me. It was poisoning me.

When I Tried to Make It Right

One day, while dropping off the kids, the weight got too heavy. I asked her to forgive me. I wasn't expecting a grand gesture, just some acknowledgement, a flicker of shared humanity.

She didn't hesitate.

"I already did."

Flat. Dismissive. Like it was old news.

It hit harder than I expected. I'd braced for anger or tears—but this? It felt like I didn't even matter anymore. Like the damage I'd done didn't deserve a second glance.

But here's the thing: even though her words didn't land the way I hoped, *asking still mattered*.

Not because it changed her. Because it began to change me.

That night, I wrote her a letter I never sent. I admitted my selfishness. My pride. My failures as a husband. I left one thing out—the most painful truth. But even naming part of it loosened the grip bitterness had on me.

Forgiveness started there, not as a single act, but as an uncomfortable movement toward the truth.

The Truth I Wasn't Ready to Say

That letter was honest, but not whole.

Because I still hadn't said the worst thing.

I'd had an affair. I never told her during the marriage. And even now, years later, I still wasn't ready to say it out loud. I kept telling myself God had already forgiven me, that it didn't matter anymore.

But it did. It mattered because until I was honest about everything, I couldn't fully forgive *myself*.

The hardest forgiveness wasn't hers. It was mine.

I'd look back on journal entries—like Day 301, where I wrote, *"A sermon on 1 Corinthians 13 showed how far I'd strayed from love."* At the time, I told myself it referred to emotional distance.

But I knew there was more beneath that line, a fracture I hadn't yet named.

That truth wouldn't surface fully until later, until Chapter 16. But the forgiveness I offered myself in this season, though incomplete, cracked the door toward healing.

Forgiveness Comes in Layers

It was slow. Uneven. Some days, I wanted peace. Other days, I wanted revenge.

But over time, a few things became clear:

- **I had to face my own heart honestly.** Not to drown in shame, but to stop pretending. I wasn't just the one left. I was also the one who had left emotionally and physically, long before the marriage ended.
- **I had to ask for forgiveness without expecting anything back.** When I asked her, it wasn't to fix things. It was time to start letting go of what I carried.
- **I had to start believing that the future could be different.** Even if the past was stained, the next chapter didn't have to be.

There's a line I wrote on Day 269: *"By focusing on the present and future, I'm beginning to rediscover who I am."* Forgiveness let me start living forward again.

A Daily Choice

Some days, I forgave easily. Other days, I rehashed old arguments in my head and came out angrier than before.

But slowly, I made forgiveness a practice:

- **I named what hurt.** On Day 115, I wrote: *"The death of those dreams feels overwhelming."* I didn't try to sound strong. I just let it be true.

- **I chose empathy.** Not to excuse what she did, but to see her humanity. That softened something in me.

- **I set boundaries.** Gossip tempted me. So did venting. My quiet line became: *"She's my kids' mom, and God will win sooner or later."* That reminder helped me honor her, even in private.

- **I prayed.** Not lofty prayers. Just whispers. "God, help her." "God, help me." Over time, those prayers rewired how I felt.

What Forgiveness Did (and Didn't) Do

Forgiveness didn't erase the pain. It didn't excuse either of our choices. It didn't make us friends or magically restore what was broken.

But it broke the chain I'd been dragging.

I once had a friend who never forgave his ex-wife. Ten years later, he was still bitter. Still telling the same stories. Still angry. Still stuck. That scared me. I didn't want to become that man.

Forgiveness didn't change the past. But it gave me a future.

What It Prepared Me For

This part of my story—this partial forgiveness, this not-yet-wholeness—set the stage for something deeper. I didn't know it then, but a time was coming when I'd finally face everything. The hidden pieces. The shame I hadn't voiced.

That's the thing about forgiveness—it prepares the soil. Makes space for truth. For healing. For the kind of freedom that doesn't come from being right, but from being *real*.

We'll get to that in Chapter 16.

But for now, know this:

Forgiveness isn't weakness. It's strength is on the slowest setting. It's the courage to stop blaming and start becoming.

And it's one of the few things that actually makes you lighter when you give it away.

Reflection Questions

- What judgment or failure have you struggled to forgive in yourself?
- Where are you still waiting for someone else to "own their part" before you let go?
- What small act of forgiveness could shift your heart today?

Practical Activity

Write a raw, unsent letter. Maybe to her. Maybe to yourself. Don't polish it. Just be real. Then pray, *"God, help me release this."* Fold it away. Burn it. Tuck it in your Bible. Let it be the beginning—not the end—of a deeper release.

Prayer

> Father, You see what I hide. You know the truths I've spoken... and the ones I still bury. Help me forgive. Not just once, but daily. Help me release the need to be right.

Show me that forgiveness isn't surrendering to the pain—it's stepping free from it. Heal the parts of me that still flinch. Make space in me for truth, for grace, and for what You still want to build. In Jesus' name, Amen.

# CHAPTER 11

FATHERHOOD AFTER DIVORCE
LOVING YOUR KIDS WELL

The house was quiet in a way it had never been before. Taylor was six. Sydney was three. Just days earlier, I'd been flipping pancakes while their laughter filled the hallway. Now I was driving them across town—back to a house I was no longer welcome in.

I still had the title *Dad*, but suddenly it felt paper-thin—hollow in the absence of their daily laughter and nighttime snuggles. The fear that haunted me most wasn't about money or failure or public opinion. It was this: *Would they still feel loved by me, even when I wasn't there?*

A Promise I Never Sent

Not long after the separation, I sat down and wrote a letter to Taylor and Sydney. I told them they were loved. That none of this was their fault. That I'd always be their daddy, on their best days and worst, whether near or far. I never gave them that letter. But I kept it as a reminder to myself. A flag in the ground. A promise I had to keep.

Then one day on the drive back to their mom's, Sydney's voice came from the back seat: "Daddy, why are you and Mommy getting a divorce?"

She was three. What answer could I give?

I swallowed hard and said something about Mommy and Daddy still loving them very much, even though we wouldn't be together. It felt inadequate—because it was. I didn't even understand it all myself. But I kept showing up. That became my pattern.

To put it in perspective, I didn't have family nearby. Most of my friends were gone too—divorce has a way of scattering people. There were moments I thought about leaving, moving back to the East Coast, where life felt familiar. If I did, I could grow my business, get back on my feet financially, maybe even start fresh somewhere with new friends and possibilities.

But every time I pictured that, I saw my daughters' faces. I couldn't bear the thought of missing out on their lives.

Looking back, staying was the best decision I ever made.

Learning to Love Without Control

At first, my anger toward my ex crept into everything. Drop-offs felt like reopening a wound. I'd bite my tongue and seeth inside, wanting her to see how much this was hurting me—and them.

But then I'd see Taylor's worried glance in the mirror. Hear Sydney's giggle, trying to lighten the mood. And it would hit me: my frustration didn't touch their mom—it only spilled over onto them.

So I drew a line. I couldn't control what happened at her house. But I could protect what happened at mine. I could protect their hearts. That became my mission.

Self-Control in a House Full of Girls

I come from a family of Italian yellers—passionate voices, strong opinions, tempers that rise before thoughts fully form. But parenting two little girls didn't leave room for that.

I had to learn to regulate myself in ways I never had before. There were times I got short with them—sure. But yelling? That didn't fly. And part of what helped was simply this: I only had them for a few days at a time. I wasn't carrying the full weight of daily parenting. I was given the gift of windows—small stretches of time where I could be present, engaged, and emotionally available. And I poured myself into those windows.

If there's any reason my girls look back and say I was a good dad, it's not because I got it all right. It's because they got the best version of me, as often as I could give it.

The Things That Helped

I didn't have a master plan. But looking back, a few things made all the difference.

1. **I Guarded Their Hearts—Even From Me**

    I never badmouthed their mom. I made it a rule. When I was tempted to vent, I'd say gently, "She's your mom and she loves you." I wanted them to be free to love her—no guilt, no confusion.

2. **I Made Room for Joy**

    From sit-n-spins in the living room to late-night dance parties during movie marathons, I made my home a place where they could be kids. Divorce had stolen enough. I wasn't going to let it steal their joy, too.

3. **I Created Traditions, Not Just Visits**

    Friday night movies. Saturday breakfast at Scramblers. Sunday morning church. These weren't just ways to fill time; they were intentional choices that anchored us. And when life felt chaotic, those simple routines gave us something to count on.

4. **I Stayed Present—Even When It Hurt**

    There were school plays where I had to sit alone next to her family. Church events where I felt like an outsider. Times when being there stung. But I showed up anyway. And over time, something unexpected happened.

Earning Back Respect

Eventually, my ex's family began to see something different. Not right away. But slowly. I believe that by showing up, loving my girls well, and staying consistent, I earned their respect again.

Years later, after both girls had graduated from high school, my former father-in-law—one of the few men I'd looked up to as a young man—pulled me aside. He looked me in the eyes and said, "I love you."

That moment still catches in my throat.

I had made a thousand mistakes. But I kept showing up. And somehow, God brought fruit out of the wreckage.

A Quiet Commitment

Throughout those years, I also made another quiet decision: I wouldn't introduce my daughters to anyone I dated unless marriage were a real possibility. And I didn't remarry until they were grown. Not by some strategic plan. It just worked out that way. Looking back, I needed more time than they did. I had so much healing to do before I could be a healthy partner to anyone else.

The Legacy

Taylor is now married with children—my grandchildren. Watching her become a wife and mother has been one of the most profound joys of my life. Her story is one of grace—of God meeting her, shaping her, and guiding her into a life filled with purpose and love. I see God's fingerprints all over her journey.

Sydney, the little girl whose voice once broke the silence of my car with questions too big for her age, grew into a bright, resilient woman. We spent hours driving together—windows down, music up—having conversations that mattered. For a time, she attended and graduated from the college where I worked, and I got to witness firsthand her strength, her wit, and that contagious smile that could light up a room.

Their hearts are kind, strong, and anchored. I see how God cared for them through the mess I couldn't clean up. And somehow, despite all I lacked, He gave them more than I could have ever asked for.

I'm not just proud of who they've become. I'm humbled. Because I know what it cost. I know what they walked through. And I know the One who walked with them. There's fruit in that. And by God's grace, I got to taste it.

Reflection Questions

- Where have you seen your brokenness impact your kids—and where has grace shown up in spite of it?
- What's one small way you could create safety and joy for your children this week?
- What's a personal rule or boundary you could set to protect their hearts?

Practical Activity

Write a letter to your children—whether they're young or grown. Don't polish it. Just speak your heart. Then consider one tradition you can start (or restart) the next time you're with them. It doesn't have to be big. Just real.

Prayer

Father, thank You for entrusting me with these children. I fall short so often. But You never do. Help me reflect Your patience, Your kindness, and Your steady love. Teach me how to be the kind of dad they can count on—not because I'm perfect, but because I'm present. Let my love anchor them, even when life feels unsteady. In Jesus' name, Amen.

CHAPTER 12
TALKING TO YOUR EX WITHOUT CONFLICT

Learning to parent after divorce wasn't just about how I showed up for my kids—it was also about how I communicated with their mom. The marriage had ended, but our roles as parents hadn't. We were still connected through our children, and every conversation carried weight.

In those early days, even the simplest exchange could feel loaded. A short text about a pickup time could stir up years of unresolved frustration. Everything felt personal, even when it wasn't meant to be.

Navigating the Emotional Minefield

My ex-wife knew exactly how to push my buttons—sometimes on purpose, most of the time without even realizing it. That's the danger of shared history. When we allow pain and hurt to lead, even the most mundane conversations can feel like landmines.

I used to replay our interactions in my head afterward—rewriting the script with better comebacks, imagining how I could have made my point louder or clearer. But every time I fought to win, I lost something more important: peace.

And worse—my kids felt it.

They didn't need more tension. They needed parents who could talk like adults. I had to learn that any emotional reaction was ever neutral—it either built something or broke something.

Learning Through Mistakes

It wasn't knowing better that changed me. It was failure.

I messed up more times than I can count. Fired off angry texts. Raised my voice on phone calls. Took the bait when silence would've been better. And I always hated how it felt afterward.

Eventually, something clicked: I didn't need to win—I needed to create stability for my daughters. That truth became the filter I tried to run every interaction through. I didn't master it. But I started aiming for it.

The Small Shifts That Helped

Here are a few changes that, over time, made all the difference:

1. **I Focused on the Problem, Not the Person**

    At first, every disagreement felt like a personal attack. But gradually, I learned to separate the issue from the history. If the girls needed something, it didn't matter who was "right"—only what served them best.

2. **I Set Boundaries (and Tried to Keep Them)**

    No late-night texts. No venting during drop-offs. No responding to emotion with more emotion. We didn't always succeed—but even small boundaries created breathing room.

3. **I Learned to Listen (Even When I Disagreed)**

    This one took time. I had to stop rehearsing my responses and actually hear what she was saying. Listening didn't mean agreeing—but it usually helped lower the temperature.

4. **I Let Some Things Go**

    I used to treat every decision like a hill worth dying on. Eventually, I realized some hills didn't matter. If it wasn't going to matter in a year, it probably wasn't worth the energy.

5. **I Reframed the Language**

    It felt awkward at first, but changing "You're always late!" to "Pickup times have been tough lately—can we fix that?"

made a difference. I failed at this often, but when I got it right, it helped.

Handling Conflict When It Came

Even with better tools, conflict didn't disappear. But I learned to respond instead of react:

- **Pause first.** Walk away, breathe, pray—then respond.
- **Stay solution-focused.** Don't rehash old arguments. Just solve the issue at hand.
- **Own your part.** Apologize when necessary. It disarms more than you'd think.

Sometimes, we'd switch to texting if things got heated. Other times, we just gave it a day. And yes, sometimes I took the high road when it felt like she didn't deserve it. But I know she did the same for me. Eventually, we became distant but functional teammates—not close friends, but peaceful co-parents.

The Moment That Changed My Perspective

I'll never forget a voicemail she left one day. The girls needed money for school clothes. I felt it rising—the frustration, the defensiveness. Wasn't that what child support was for?

I almost fired back with a snarky text. But I paused.

And in that pause, I remembered: those were my daughters. This wasn't about her. It was about them.

I called back, asked what they needed, and sent the money. Not because I had to. Because I wanted to. That shift—from defensiveness to purpose—began to reshape our communication.

Peace Isn't About Agreement

I used to think peace meant finally getting along or agreeing on everything. But peace came in a different form. It came through restraint. Through clarity. By putting the girls above my pride.

Over time, things softened. We didn't become close, but we became steady. Our daughters knew we were still a united front in what mattered.

Respect Where It's Due

And here's something it took me time to understand: the only way two divorced people can truly be good parents is by finding some common ground—some thread of appreciation for the part the other parent plays. You don't have to be friends. You don't have to agree on everything. But you do have to respect the effort the other person is making for your kids. It changes the temperature. It changes the whole dynamic.

Whatever healing I found, whatever stability I built—it mattered, but it wasn't the whole story. The reason our girls grew up steady and loved is because she was doing her part, too. They needed both of us showing up in our own ways, even when we were broken, even when we didn't get along. And that's a truth I fully appreciate now.

Reflection Questions

- ⊃ What triggers the most conflict in your conversations with your ex?
- ⊃ Which boundaries or habits could help lower tension?

⮕ Where can you practice restraint, even when you feel justified to react?

Practical Activity

Write down three recurring topics that tend to spark conflict. For each, brainstorm a neutral response or calming phrase you can use next time. Then ask God to help you speak from strength, not ego.

Prayer

Father, You see the conversations that leave me drained and defensive. Help me guard my words. Let peace—not pride—guide my voice. Teach me to protect my kids not just from conflict, but from my own unchecked reactions. Help me take the high road, even when it feels unfair. You are my defender and my guide. In Jesus' name, Amen.

CHAPTER 13

THE FINANCIAL STORM THE COLLAPSE THAT SAVED ME

Divorce stripped me bare, but losing my family was just the beginning. What followed was a slow unraveling—a downward spiral where I'd lose nearly everything else: my business, my home, my reputation, my money, and worst of all, my sense of identity. It wasn't just losing things; it was losing the version of myself I thought made me worthy of love and respect.

To the outside world, I appeared successful. I owned a thriving business, drove luxury cars, had a boat on the lake, and lived in a picture-perfect home in a nice neighborhood. I looked like a man who had figured it all out. But underneath, I was hollow, drowning in pride and desperate for validation. And I was spending recklessly to keep up the image.

When the Facade Crumbled

After the divorce, instead of stepping back and regrouping, I doubled down on appearances. I moved into a flashier office in the most prestigious building in town, leased an even nicer car, and threw money at ventures driven by ego instead of wisdom. I wasn't investing, I was performing. I wanted people to see me and think, *He's still winning.* Every financial decision was fueled by pride and pain.

I threw money at dating, too—expensive dinners, gifts, events—all a thinly veiled attempt to prove to myself that I was still desirable. That I could still "get" someone. That I still mattered. But like everything else, it was a mask. Money wasn't about romance. It was about numbing the rejection and filling the silence where intimacy used to live.

But that hole only got deeper. Every flashy purchase was like pouring water into a bucket full of holes. The feeling faded immediately, leaving me emptier than before.

By 2007, it started catching up to me. I sold the profitable part of the company—a deal that looked like a win on paper. I kept operating what remained, but I never adjusted my lifestyle. I was still spending like that level of income was permanent, still clinging to the image.

Then came the 2008 crash, and everything unraveled. By 2012, I was bankrupt. The business collapsed. My house went into foreclosure. My possessions vanished one by one.

I had lost everything I once used to define my worth: my marriage, my business, my house, my status, my image. Everything I thought made me a man was gone. I remember clearly the night before the bank sold the house at foreclosure—walking room to room, empty walls echoing with memories I couldn't hold onto anymore.

A Night I'll Never Forget

That night in the house—the final night—it all hit me. I wasn't just losing a structure. I was watching the last symbol of control crumble.

This was the home God had provided for me after the divorce. It had once felt redemptive. A safe place. And I had squandered it like the prodigal son—through pride, performance, and reckless spending.

I sat in the dark on a bare floor, weeping. Not the quiet kind, but the soul-breaking kind. I gasped for air between sobs, asking questions I didn't know if God would answer.

Are You even there?
Do You even care?

Romans 8:31 flickered in my mind—"If God is for us, who can be against us?" But that night, it felt like the opposite. God felt distant, maybe because I had wandered so far.

And then the quiet truth hit me: I had built my entire identity on sand. On wealth. On status. On the performance of being okay. And it was all gone—all of it.

Slowly Learning to Live Again

Recovery wasn't quick or clean. My pride didn't disappear overnight—it was slowly dismantled, one painful realization at a time.

I took a basic desk job. Humbled. Paying child support and living paycheck to paycheck. But at night, I hustled, trying to rebuild fragments of what I'd lost. My ego still fought for attention, tempting me to slip back into appearances and overspending.

But God kept sending grace.

One of the clearest examples was my friend Jason. He had been there *before* the collapse—we had built companies together, chased pride together, and lost a few things together. But through it all, his loyalty never wavered. When the bankruptcy hit, and everything crumbled, he didn't distance himself. He stuck closer than a brother.

Post-collapse, we started more ventures together—a car dealership, a few side projects—nothing glamorous, but solid, honest work. More than anything, we just liked working and being around each other. His friendship gave me stability in a time when everything else felt like shifting ground. He got married and started a family, and while life changed for both of us, that bond remained.

And then came one of the many small but profound graces: when I lost the house and had no credit, our business was leasing a commercial building next to some downtown lofts. The same owners owned the lofts next door and let me rent one without a credit check. I lived there for over seven years. When I didn't have a car, guess what? We owned a car dealership. I could drive what I needed. It wasn't flashy—but it was God's provision, plain and simple.

I began to find my footing again. Not in wealth or image, but in living within my means. In showing up. In being generous, even when I had almost nothing.

But something in me still held back. I was surviving—but not truly trusting. I had seen God provide through friendships and open doors, yet deep down, I was still afraid to surrender fully.

Trusting God with Pennies

After bankruptcy, I stopped giving. I told myself it was wise stewardship. The truth? I was scared. I kept a small savings buffer—just a few thousand dollars—just in case. But that money never grew. It never moved. It just sat there, like a monument to my fear.

After heading back to church again (Chapter 15), I connected with a new friend, Justin. Like Jason, Justin is an all-in kind of guy. He challenges you without saying much. Around that time, our church invited people to give toward a ministry need. I told Justin, "I'm not doing that. The mega church doesn't need my money."

But Justin didn't argue. He just said, "Try God. See what He'll do."

I remembered sitting in that same church years earlier, giving my last few dollars, praying desperately for rescue from losing everything, and feeling like God had gone silent. That experience left a scar. But Justin's challenge stirred something deeper. Maybe this wasn't about money. Maybe this was about trust.

So I wrote a check, not out of guilt. Not to impress. But out of trust and surrender.

Something shifted not just in my wallet, but in my spirit. I wasn't giving to get—I was giving to honor God. To say, *I trust You again*. And wouldn't you know it? Small, unexpected provision started showing up. Checks in the mail. Side gigs I hadn't pursued. Opportunities I couldn't explain. Not flashy. But faithful.

Everything I have today was born from that obedience, not to wealth, but to trust. And trust is richer than any bank account I've ever held.

What I didn't fully see then—but do now—is that this was part of the greater healing God was working in me. Spiritual, emotional, physical, and now financial. The Big Four. Each had been shattered. Each had to be rebuilt. And this chapter—learning to trust God again with money, with provision, with stability—was the beginning of financial healing that finally went deeper than numbers in a bank account.

Lessons Learned the Hard Way

I wish I hadn't had to lose everything to learn these truths. But maybe my story can help you avoid the same painful path. Here's what I took away:

- **Money can't heal emotional wounds.** No amount of wealth or success fills the void left by broken relationships or spiritual emptiness. It just delays the pain long enough for it to grow wild—until it consumes everything.

- **Appearances deceive, but honesty frees you.** Keeping up a facade eventually collapses. Facing the truth, no matter how ugly, is the only road to real freedom.

- **Money won't win the right woman.** It may attract attention, but often from those seeking validation, just like I was. True love isn't bought; it's built through honesty, humility, and being exactly who God made you to be. When you walk in that truth, the right woman—God's woman—will see your worth, not your wallet.

- **Generosity always returns multiplied.** Giving, even when you have little, enriches your life in ways money never can.

- **Humility opens doors that pride never could.** Admitting mistakes, asking for help, and living within your means sets you free from the weight of false pride.

- **Real friendships have nothing to do with wealth.** True friends stay through the wreckage, loving you regardless of status or success.

- **Trust God's daily provision.** When everything else failed, God provided enough day by day. His faithfulness was stronger than my worst fears.

What Real Success Looks Like Now

Today, my life looks nothing like it once did—and I'm deeply grateful for that.

Yet, the biggest shift isn't visible. It's internal—the understanding that who I am is more important than what I own or what my title is. My worth is defined by God's grace, not my achievements.

Losing everything financially, like divorce, was painful beyond words. But God used that loss to show me what truly matters.

He rebuilt my life from scratch—not into a return to outward success, but into something deeper, richer, and far more lasting.

If you're struggling financially or tempted by appearances after divorce, please know this: success isn't what you own. It isn't your income, your house, or the image you project. Your identity is found in Christ—steady, unshaken, and not tied to what can be taken from you. Real success is how you live, who you love, and the authenticity with which you walk before God.

Reflection Questions

- How has pride or fear driven your financial choices since divorce?
- Where might God be inviting you to greater humility and trust right now?
- What's one honest, humble step you can take toward healthier finances today?

Practical Activity

Write down where pride, ego, or appearances are influencing your financial decisions. Beside each, note a practical, humble alternative you can embrace. Pray for the courage to live out those wiser choices daily.

Prayer

> Father, financial strain has a way of exposing what I trust most. Show me where pride, fear, or the need to appear "put together" has shaped my decisions. Forgive me for tying my worth to money, success, or control. Teach me humility, honesty, and wise stewardship—especially when the path forward feels uncertain. Lead me away from ego-driv-

en choices and toward what truly lasts. Help me trust Your daily provision more than my own ability to manage outcomes. Rebuild my heart so my life honors You, not just my balance sheet. In Jesus' name, Amen.

CHAPTER

14

DATING AGAIN WHEN HEALING COMES FIRST

After divorce, dating feels like the next obvious step. You lose your person, your rhythm, your companion—so it's natural to want someone in your life again. I sure did. But if you're anything like me, what you want and what you're actually ready for aren't always the same thing.

After she left, it didn't take long before I was in someone else's bed, someone else's arms, someone else's life. I wasn't out to hurt anyone, but I was hurting—and that made me dangerous in ways I didn't fully understand. I'd get into a relationship that would last three, six, maybe nine months—then disappear into a long stretch of solitude, convincing myself I was doing better. I wasn't. I was cycling between numbness and need, bouncing between feeling lonely and proving to myself I still had it.

I wanted intimacy, but didn't know how to be emotionally intimate. I wanted connection but hadn't faced the parts of me that kept sabotaging it. The Big Four—my spiritual walk, emotional health, physical well-being, and financial stability—were all cracked. But I didn't realize how deep the damage went until I kept hurting good women who deserved more than the version of me they got.

When I was done dating, I got really good at making women break up with me. I'm not proud of that. But I'd pick at what they didn't like about me—habits, attitudes, opinions—and lean into those things until they left. It felt easier than facing the truth. It was cowardly, but it gave me a false sense of control. Hurting people hurt people, and I was still hurting.

Truth is, I didn't believe I was worthy of real love. So when someone started to love me, I'd test it. I'd push and sabotage and self-destruct. I told myself I was being cautious—protecting myself from pain—but I was just afraid. Afraid that if they saw the real me, they'd leave. So I forced their hand before they ever got the chance.

Looking back, those breakups weren't really about them. They were about a man who didn't know his own value. Until I believed I had worth, I kept giving myself away to people and things that only degraded who God created me to be.

When You're Not Ready, But They Are

Years after the divorce, I met someone who fit. She was kind, godly, and steady. She was ready for the kind of life I thought I wanted—but I wasn't. I was struggling through a financial collapse, trying to keep my head above water. Emotionally, I was still spinning in cycles of guilt, pride, and shame. Spiritually, I was saying the right words, but I was living a disconnected life. That relationship slipped away—not because she wasn't right, but because I wasn't.

A few months later, I found out she was engaged and then married. Initially, that hurt me in a way I didn't see coming. But I was so numb, I just went back to repeating the same poor choices and mistakes. God gave me so many chances to change without pain, but each time, I kept choosing pain. It was comfortable. It felt familiar.

By that time, everything was falling apart. The financial storm you read about in the last chapter was playing out in real time, while I was still dating. Still grasping at ego. Still chasing the illusion. So I just moved on to the next date. The next girl. The next hurt. The next poor choice.

By 2016, I finally reached a place where I didn't want to live like that anymore. I stopped dating at the beginning of the year. But by midyear, I thought I had met the one. She fit almost everything I thought I wanted. But I still wasn't the man I knew I could be. Still selfish. Still out for myself.

That relationship ended quickly. And I knew—she was my last date until God healed me fully. I finally drew the line in the sand.

That moment marked a shift: I had to stop pretending I was ready and get serious about what healing actually required.

Stabilizing the Big Four

Throughout the book, I mentioned the Big Four—spiritual, emotional, physical, and financial health. At the time, I didn't realize how shattered each area really was. But to truly heal, I had to return to them—not just in theory, but in practice.

I couldn't fully stabilize these areas while I was actively dating. Every relationship distracted me from the deeper work I needed to do. It wasn't until I stopped dating altogether and chose purity that I finally got serious about becoming whole.

And I don't just mean sexual purity. I mean emotional purity, too. I stopped entertaining attention from people I knew weren't meant for me. I stopped needing the high. I stopped trying to fill the silence.

Here's how each of those four areas began to change:

- **Spiritually**: I began to lean into God—not for what He could give me, but to finally discover who He created me to be. I returned to Scripture, to prayer, to community, and to honesty. I stopped just attending church and started letting it change me. I prayed for forgiveness and asked God to break the soul ties formed through all the disobedience.

- **Emotionally**: I got real about my past. From being homeless as a tween to losing everything as an adult, I sat in counseling sessions that tore me apart and rebuilt me piece by piece. I grieved my marriage. I grieved who I had become. I grieved the masks I had worn. And I let it go.

- **Physically**: I started taking care of my body—not to attract someone new, but because I wanted to be strong for whatever came next. Exercise, rest, and healthier choices all became part of honoring the life I had left.

- **Financially**: I learned to live within my means. No more flashy cars. No more ego-driven ventures. No more spending to feel something. Simplicity became healing.

Should I Date?

That's the question so many ask.

Early on, I had a twisted theology—I thought, *Maybe I can't get married again because I am divorced, but I can date... and I'll ask for forgiveness later.* That mindset kept me stuck, hurting myself and others in the process.

My friend Jason had a different approach. He took dating seriously, dating with the intention of marriage. He honored the women he spent time with and honored God with his intentions. His story unfolded much differently than mine. He experienced the fruit of God's plan for his life more than a decade before I did.

Wherever you land on whether you can date or should date, I've learned this: it's always wiser to take care of your Big Four first.

Lean into God. Let Him restore you after the windfall of divorce so that when you do date—if you date—you're making decisions from a place of healing, not hunger.

Everyone has an opinion about when you can date again. Some people say you should wait three months for every year you were married. I'm not sure how accurate that is—or if it works at all—but what I do know is this: Securing your Big Four will almost always create the space and time for real healing and honest reflection.

Choosing God sooner, I believe, aligns you quicker with God's plan. I didn't. And it cost me years.

That doesn't mean God can't redeem it—He absolutely did. But Jason's story reminds me that obedience doesn't just protect us. It positions us.

Until You Know Your Worth

Here's what I learned the hard way:

1. Until you believe you have worth, you will keep giving yourself away to people and things that only degrade who God created you to be.

2. If you don't know who you are in Christ, you'll hand your identity to the next person who smiles at you. You'll compromise. You'll perform. You'll beg for scraps when God is preparing a table.

But when you lean into God—when you make Him the center—everything shifts.

> *"Seek first the Kingdom of God and His righteousness, and all these things will be added to you."*
> **—Matthew 6:33**

That verse wasn't a theory but became my mantra. I wasn't going to settle—or let someone else settle—for the half-healed version of me they met.

I wanted to become the best version of me for the future God had in store. Whether that meant being single the rest of my life or marrying again, there was no in-between.

Taking Practical Steps Forward

When the time finally came to open my heart again, I walked into it with clear eyes and a steady spirit. My motives were different. My posture was different.

Here's what helped me take that step with intention:

- Reflect and define what you're really looking for. Write it down. Pray over it. Know what matters and what doesn't.
- Be willing to surrender what you want for what God has. His plans are always better than anything you can script.
- Ask God to filter your heart, not just your inbox. Pray for the wisdom to walk away when something isn't right.
- Build a life worth sharing, not just a dating profile.
- Date with marriage in mind. No games. No hidden agendas.
- Be honest early—about your story, your healing, your boundaries, and your faith.
- Communicate clearly. Say the hard things. Silence builds walls faster than honesty ever will.
- Guard your purity—not out of shame, but because your heart is sacred.

Why I Waited—and What I Gained

People asked me why I waited so long, why I stopped dating entirely for years. The truth? I didn't want to keep hurting people. And I didn't want to keep hurting myself.

I needed time not just to recover, but to become who I was meant to be. I had to know God was enough, even if I never married again. I had to want God more than I wanted a relationship.

During that season, I encountered some remarkable women. But they weren't mine. They were someone else's future, and I didn't want to get in the way of that. When you walk closely with God, you notice the red flags sooner. The absence of peace is enough.

She Came Along

When I wasn't looking anymore, she showed up. We met for coffee over an article I had written for *Single Christianity Magazine*, which had a profound impact on her. Neither of us was there for a date. But there was something about her. Kind. God-centered. No games. No second-guessing.

We both knew who we were. We knew what we wanted. And most of all, we knew Who we were following. I can say this now, but I knew almost immediately: she was my person.

For the first time in my life, I experienced what it meant to love and be loved in a healthy way. Grounded in truth. Fueled by peace. Anchored in purpose.

And yes—it was worth the wait. More than five years in at the writing of this book, and it's more than I could ask for or imagine. But we'll talk more about that in later chapters.

Dating Has Changed

Let's be honest: dating today is a mess. If you don't have guardrails, you will get dragged into something you weren't planning. Dating without healing leads to regret. Dating without clarity leads to confusion. Every time.

That's why I say this now with confidence:

Don't date unless you're healed. Don't date unless you're ready. Don't date unless you've made peace with being single.

Because when you reach that place—when you're walking closely with God—you'll know what to do. You'll know what's real. And you'll wait for the one who sees your heart and says, "I've been praying for you too."

Reflection Questions

- Have you dated to heal, prove something, or escape loneliness?
- What would it look like to pursue purity and wait on God's timing?
- Are you becoming the kind of person you hope to attract?

Practical Activity

Write a journal entry titled: "Who I'm Becoming."
List the qualities you're cultivating in yourself—and the kind of person you believe God is preparing you to meet. Then write a prayer over both.

Prayer

God, You see it all—every wound, every longing, every mistake. Forgive me for the times I chased the world's love instead of healing. Break any soul ties that were created by living outside Your plan. Teach me to be whole in You. Help me wait—not with bitterness, but with hope. Shape me into someone who loves well, who sees clearly, who walks in truth. And when the time is right, lead me to someone who reflects Your heart. In Jesus' name, Amen.

# CHAPTER 15
THE LINE IN THE SAND

One particular Sunday, I decided to go back to church. It had been a while since I'd gone consistently.

In Chapter 1, I talked about sitting in the car and praying, "I need You, God. Help me." This was that day.

I was wrestling with going in—sitting alone, navigating the awkward smiles and small talk. It felt like effort. Like buying a lottery ticket, where the odds of something good happening were stacked against me.

But I went anyway.

I took a seat in the middle section near the sound booth. I remember it like it was yesterday.

I wasn't fully present. My guard was still up. I knew how to blend in—I'd been around church long enough to fake it. But inside, I felt disconnected, like I was trying to re-enter a world I'd only watched from the sidelines for too long.

Then it happened.

A video began playing on the screen. And there he was—a guy I knew from my tech business. We'd crossed paths back in the party days, and he was a mess back then, too. But now, he was talking about how God had changed his life. He had a wife. Kids. A life. Peace.

He wasn't just surviving—he was thriving. Not because life was perfect, but because something inside him had changed. Something real.

And it hit me.

That quiet prayer I'd whispered in the car wasn't just desperation. It was the start of surrender. Something had tried to keep me out of that church. But I'd made it in. And what I saw on that screen wasn't just a testimony. It was a mirror.

I didn't cry. I didn't walk down an aisle. I didn't drop to my knees.

I just whispered:

> *"God, if You can do that in him... surely You can do it in me. Forgive me. Come back into my life and change me."*

That prayer—that moment of honesty—was my spiritual line in the sand.

And one word echoed in my heart:

Obedience.

Not church attendance.
Not looking the part.
Obedience.

I Knew God, But I Wasn't Following Him

I had called myself a Christian most of my life. I'd checked the boxes. But if I was honest, I was doing it all on my terms.

I gave God the appearance of surrender, but not the reality.

Even after my divorce, after the collapse of my finances and identity, I was still trying to control the narrative. I chased comfort. I chased women. I chased money. I knew how to survive. But I hadn't learned yet how to yield.

I hadn't learned how to surrender.

Everything I had built in the years after divorce—business, success, validation, relationships—crumbled. Yet part of me still believed I could rebuild it all myself. Watching that man on the screen shattered that illusion.

Because for the first time, I saw someone who wasn't faking it. And I realized—I didn't want to rebuild my life.

I wanted a new one.

Surrender Is the Starting Line

Change didn't come when I figured something out. It came when I couldn't fake it anymore. When I got tired—deep soul tired—of the way things were.

Tired of the cycle.
Tired of the double life.
Tired of knowing about God without actually following Him.

That day, sitting in a sea of strangers, I drew a line in the sand. And with a whispered prayer, I surrendered.

Not in strength—but in exhaustion.

Blessing Follows Obedience

That word—*obedience*—became an anchor for me.

It didn't mean losing myself. It meant losing my need to control everything. It meant laying down relationships I knew weren't God's best. It meant leaving behind the scenes and habits that had defined my old life.

It meant saying:

> "God, whatever You want—even if it costs me."

And it did cost me. It cost me my pride. It cost me the stories I told myself. It cost me the version of me I'd been protecting for years.

But it also freed me.

Because once I let go, I could finally receive. Peace. Clarity. Healing.

That moment of surrender was the spiritual hinge on which everything else turned.

The Big Four—my emotional, physical, financial, and especially spiritual health—couldn't truly stabilize until I stopped living for myself and started walking in obedience. This wasn't about performance. It was about posture.

A Simple Faith

That Sunday wasn't the day I found religion. It was the day I finally trusted the One I'd talked about for years but never really surrendered to.

Because believing about Jesus isn't the same as believing in Him.

Even the demons believe He exists—they just don't trust Him. They don't surrender.

Real faith is more than acknowledgment; it's dependence. It's handing over the controls and admitting you're done running your life on your own terms.

Ephesians 2:8–9 says, "For it is by grace you have been saved, through faith—and this is not from yourselves, it is the gift of God—not by works, so that no one can boast."

Faith is simple, but it isn't shallow. It's trusting that Jesus' death and resurrection are enough—and choosing to stop negotiating the terms of obedience.

That day, I didn't clean myself up or promise to do better. I just stopped pretending. I finally admitted I needed saving—and let God meet me there.

What Happened Next

That kind of faith changes everything.

Not because anything was earned, but because I finally let go.

Salvation didn't arrive as a finish line—it began as trust and kept growing through surrender, day by day, step by step.

Not perfect obedience. Just consistent dependence.

And when I stumbled—and I still do—the same Jesus who saved me is the One who lifts me.

That's where real freedom lives.

That's where hope begins.

Reflection Questions

- What parts of your life are you still trying to control?
- Have you ever fully trusted Jesus with your heart—not just believed, but surrendered? If not, what's holding you back?
- What would it look like to draw your own line in the sand today

Practical Activity

Find a quiet place this week. No distractions. No phone. Just you and God.
Speak honestly—no big words, no filters.
Ask Him:

"What does surrender look like for me right now?"
Then write down whatever comes. Even a single sentence is a place to start.

Prayer

God, I've tried everything—and I'm still hurting, still restless, still searching. I don't want to do this on my own anymore. I trust You. I surrender my heart, my future, my fear, my control. Teach me what it means to walk with You in faith and obedience. Remind me I don't have to be perfect—just honest. Thank You for meeting me here. Amen.

CHAPTER

16

CHOOSING PURITY AFTER FAILURE

After surrendering, everything began to change.

Something in me had shifted. I had drawn a line in the sand with God, not just with my life, but with my identity, my desires, and my constant need to control outcomes. That surrender began to touch places I hadn't faced honestly in years, especially my sexuality.

This isn't the chapter I wanted to write. It's deeply personal, and it reveals just how broken I really was. These are the kinds of things we're taught to keep hidden. As men, we're told to push through, to figure it out ourselves, to deal with it in silence.

But silence never healed me.

The only way I could start to heal was by dragging the truth into the light—no matter how much it embarrassed me, no matter who it disappointed, and no matter how much I wanted to protect my image.

Because for men like us—men who've walked through divorce and tried to piece their lives back together—this is often the area that stays fractured the longest. Sexuality doesn't vanish when the divorce papers are signed. If anything, it becomes louder In the quiet. And when we don't talk about it honestly, shame moves in, digs deep, and keeps us stuck.

I lived in that shame for years.

Sex had always been a powerful force in my life—sometimes beautiful, more often distorted. When my marriage ended, I carried with me not just grief and regret, but years of unmet need and a warped view of sex and love. I didn't know how to bring that mess to God. I didn't even know how to face it myself.

So I did what a lot of us do.
I tried to fill the void.

From the day of my divorce until the line in the sand, I lived selfishly. I dated. I slept around. I chased connections without healing. I wanted to feel whole again, but all I ever felt was momentarily wanted, then empty again. I swung between long stretches of solitude and short-term flings. I'd pray one night and watch porn the next. I asked God for healing while refusing to surrender the parts of me I didn't want Him to touch. I figured if I ignored it, He might too. I believed people could fill me and fix me. So, my body count went up while my value went down.

That wasn't freedom. That was bondage.

The Wound I Never Faced

My first exposure to pornography came when I was eight years old. I found some magazines hidden under my older brother's bed. I didn't know what I was looking at, but it planted something in me. That seed followed me into adulthood, shaping how I saw women, how I pursued intimacy, and how I measured my worth.

In my twenties, I assumed marriage would fix it. I thought once I had a wife, the temptation would go away. It didn't. Marriage doesn't heal what's hidden—it only reveals it.

Eventually, that distortion took me somewhere I should've never gone.

I had an affair.

It was short, but the wound it left wasn't.

For years, I told no one, not my ex-wife, not my friends, not even myself in any honest way. I buried it, performed around it, tried to outpace the shame it created.

Years after the divorce, I finally told her. I thought maybe the truth would help her find closure. I hoped it would bring me peace. But it didn't do either. She was in a serious relationship at the time, and all it did was bring her more pain.

Still, I had to speak it. I had to bring it into the light. Whether or not it changed anything, it was the only way to stop hiding from myself. I was an adulterer. Pretending it wasn't true didn't undo it. But naming it—maybe that would be the beginning of healing.

Not because it made things better. But because it was in the light. And it made things honest.

Still Slipping

Even after that confession, nothing really changed. I still struggled. Still dated. Still had sex. Still watched porn. Still felt disgusted with myself.

I didn't think purity applied to me anymore. I was damaged goods. What was left to protect?

So I lived in the numbness of filling moments.

But deep down, I knew I was eroding my soul.

Each relationship was another attempt to prove I wasn't broken. Each breakup just confirmed that I still was.

The Final Piece

Looking back now, this was the last area God had to touch. First came the divorce—the emotional collapse that stripped away my identity. Then came the financial storm—the season when I lost the business, the house, and the image I'd built. Now came the hidden things—the parts no one else could see.

God had taken me through it all, and now He was putting His hand here. Nothing was left untouched. Everything had to change. Everything had to be rebuilt.

If you don't choose to change, a God who loves you will still lead you there. For me, it was slow and deliberate—like He was pulling one block at a time from a Jenga tower—until it all fell. And when it did, I couldn't keep pretending.

Drawing the Sexual Line

By 2017, I stopped dating. I stopped having sex.

The surrender you read about in the last chapter—just a few months earlier—had cracked something open. It led to a deeper letting go, the kind that touches the parts you cling to the most. The things I thought I couldn't live without. The things I used to numb the pain, distract myself, or feel like a man again.

After another relationship fell apart, I hit a wall. I realized I couldn't keep living like this—jumping from one connection to the next, hoping something would finally stick. I wasn't ready for love. Not really. Not until I got serious about the man I was becoming.

So I made a decision: I would stop it all.

No more casual relationships. No more chasing connections to feel validated. No more sex.

I drew another line in the sand—one that governed how I lived with my body, my emotions, and my sexuality.

From that moment on, I decided I would not sleep with anyone again. I would live in obedience to God, no matter what the future held.

I also quit porn. And yes, I slipped. But this time, I didn't hide. I didn't pretend it wasn't happening. I told someone. I got accountable. I stood up, spoke it out loud, and let trusted men walk with me through the mess.

I also got serious with God about the ties my past choices had created. One night, I prayed quietly, soberly—calling out each relationship, each mistake, some I could remember, others I couldn't—and I asked God to sever those unhealthy bonds. I confessed the sins, renounced the ties, and asked Him to restore what had been fractured. I told God not just what I'd done, but how deeply it had embedded itself in me. And I asked Him to undo the damage.

This wasn't mystical or magical; it was a simple, desperate act of faith. A recognition that sex touches more than just our bodies—it touches our souls (1 Corinthians 6:16–17). And when it's misused, it leaves deep pain God can—and wants to—heal.

Around that same time, both of my daughters were becoming young women. Watching them grow up shifted something in me. I couldn't unsee it. Every woman I passed on the street wasn't just a body or a smile—she was somebody's daughter—someone's little girl. And one day, someone would fall in love with mine.

And I had to ask myself: What kind of man did I want them to meet? What kind of father did I want to be remembered as?

God didn't just convict me. He surrounded me. He gave me companions.

Justin was one of them. We were walking through the same season in 2016, and the way he pursued purity stood out to me. He didn't preach it—he lived it. Quiet. Steady. Real. Seeing him choose to honor God over the world's noise pulled something forward in me. I leaned into that friendship, and we started walking that path together.

Purity Wasn't a Loss

The world says, "Try before you buy. What if the sex is bad? What if you're not compatible? It's no big deal." But it is.

When I chose purity, I had no idea I'd marry again. I assumed that season of my life was over. Religion had already told me I was disqualified. I figured I'd spend the rest of my life honoring God as a single man—and honestly, I had made peace with that.

But God had other plans.

When Kara and I met years later, I had already drawn the line. We didn't sleep together. We waited until our wedding night.

And no—I wasn't nervous. Because when you've lived in chaos and tasted surrender, peace becomes more powerful than performance.

That night, standing in our bedroom as her husband, I didn't feel deprived.

I felt peace. I felt seen. I felt loved.

Purity wasn't a sacrifice. It was a gift.

Purity Is a Fight

Let's be clear: I'm not perfect.

There were days I felt angry for no reason. Days I wanted to escape so badly, it felt physical. What I didn't realize back then was that porn and sex had become my coping mechanism. When I removed it, all the stuff I hadn't dealt with came bubbling up. And I had to face it.

This world celebrates porn, casual sex, and even affairs like they're milestones of liberation. But when the screen goes dark and the room gets quiet, all you're left with is regret.

I used to think purity was just about avoiding sin. Now I see it's about pursuing a life aligned with God's will—truth, integrity, and love. That yielded peace I hadn't known. A confidence I hadn't felt. I stopped feeling fragmented. My thoughts became clearer. My heart steadied. I felt free, not just from lust, but from the chaos it had brought into every part of my life.

Filling the Void

You can't just remove sin. You have to replace it with something better.

Let's be real—religion often say, "Just fill it with God," but rarely explain what that actually means. For me, it started simply. I read my Bible. I started praying again. I served. Those small things reconnected me to who God is—and slowly, I began to see Him more clearly and, in some ways, become more like Him.

I got back into serving, leading a small group of singles who were also trying to find their way. I joined the church's welcome team, where I shook hands and greeted people on Sundays. I started working out again with Justin and a few other friends. I got active. I got honest.

And over time, the Big Four—my spiritual, emotional, physical, and financial health—began to align again.

That was the difference.

Purity isn't about perfection. It's about refusing to hide anymore. Even now, years into walking in freedom, the enemy still whispers, "You're still that guy." But I'm not.

There are still days I feel the tug. I see something online, and part of me wants to pause. To look a little longer. But I know where that road leads.

That's what purity looks like now. Not spotless—but surrendered.

And here's the truth: just because you surrender something doesn't mean you won't struggle with it again. It just means you've decided not to live there anymore.

Proverbs 24:16 says, "Though the righteous fall seven times, they rise again."

So I'll keep rising.

What Helped Me Rebuild

Again, no formula. But here's what helped:

- **Honest confession.** I didn't just confess to God—I told my trusted friends. I told Jason when I slipped. I told Justin when I struggled. That honesty created space for grace.
- **Practical boundaries.** I stopped watching certain shows. I deleted apps. I said no to late-night texts. I made it inconvenient to sin.
- **Real accountability.** I surrounded myself with men who weren't afraid to ask hard questions. "Have you looked at porn?" was often asked.

- **Scripture.** I let it rewire my mind. I wrote verses on notecards and kept them nearby. One of my anchors was 1 Corinthians 6:20—"You were bought at a price. Therefore, honor God with your body."
- **A better question.** I stopped asking, "What am I giving up?" and started asking, "What kind of man am I becoming?"

For the Man Who Thinks It's Too Late

Maybe you've already blown it. Maybe you've given yourself away more times than you can count.

I get it. I've been there.

But hear me—
You are not too far gone.

Purity isn't about where you've been. It's about where you're going.

It's not about shame. It's about freedom.
It's not about perfection. It's about obedience.
It's not just about God—it's about the man you'll become when you let Him redeem what you thought was lost.

You don't have to hide anymore. You don't have to keep circling the same old pain.

Draw your line.
And don't walk it alone.

Reflection Questions

- Where have shame or secrecy kept you stuck?
- What would it look like to draw your own purity line?

⊃ Who can walk with you in this part of the journey?

Practical Activity

Write down three things you're still carrying—shame, regret, or secrets. Then write down three people you could be honest with. Reach out to one of them this week. Open the door.

Prayer

God, I'm tired of pretending. I've made choices that broke me and hurt others. But I believe You can redeem even this. I give You my past, my pain, and my patterns. Help me walk in honesty, integrity, and purity. Give me courage to open up, strength to change, and hope to believe again. Make me new. In Jesus' name, Amen.

CHAPTER
17
REMARRIAGE: GOD'S TIMING & YOUR CALLING

By the end of 2019, life felt steadier than it had in years. The Big Four—spiritual, emotional, physical, and financial health—were finally aligned. I was serving regularly, surrounded by a strong core of friends, both men and women. Financially, it was my strongest year yet.

That December, as I prayed over what word would define the coming year, one rose to the surface: *Prepare.* I didn't know what I was preparing for, but I knew enough by now not to dismiss it. I tightened the financial reins, stocked up on essentials, and took a conservative approach to the year—but still believed 2020 would be even better than 2019.

Then, just as quietly, I sensed another impression: *You will meet and marry your wife this year.* I didn't write it on a billboard or tell the world. I held it loosely, open to it being from God, but careful not to try to make it happen in my own strength.

What I didn't know was that the year ahead would carry more change, loss, and joy than any single year in my life.

If I Don't See You Here, I'll See You in Heaven

A few months later, in February, curiosity got the better of me and I opened a dating site. Five minutes in, the old hopelessness crept back. This wasn't it. I shut the laptop and never went back.

Life moved forward. I finished my MBA the first week in March. Sixteen days later, we got the news: my mom had passed away.

Even now, I can see her smile and hear her voice. Losing her pulled something deep out of me—a tenderness I didn't realize was still buried under old layers of self-protection. It reminded me that time is not guaranteed. It stripped away my illusion that there's always *"someday"* to make things right.

That day made me see relationships differently. It made me pray differently. And strangely, it was part of God's preparation.

Nine days later, the world shut down.

Covid Lockdown Life

While fear and uncertainty swept across the globe, my small circle of friends found an unexpected rhythm. One friend had a pool, and every weekend we'd grill out, watch church on Sunday mornings, and laugh like we hadn't in years. I bought a bike and started riding.

Life, for the first time in a long time, felt light.

And then came the matchmaker.

The Matchmaker

There was a woman I knew through church circles who had followed my *Single Christianity* articles for years. She started playing matchmaker, sending me and Justin photos of her single friends. One of those pictures—more than once—was Kara.

I'd actually seen Kara before. In 2018, we sat two seats apart at a singles Christmas event. At the time, someone asked me if I wanted to get married again. I told them I didn't think so—I was still too selfish. Kara was right there, but she was praying then that God would "hide" her until the right person came along. Candidly, I didn't really see her then—because I wasn't ready to be the right person yet.

By May 2020, the matchmaker became more insistent. She crossed some personal boundaries, and I sent her a direct but respectful message asking her to stop. She didn't take it well.

She shared my message with others, twisted my words, and even tried to contact my ex-wife to damage my reputation.

In the past, that kind of attack would've sent me into defensive overdrive. But I'd learned the hard way to let God be my defender. And He was. People I never expected stood up for me, including my ex-wife. The truth rose to the surface without me having to force it.

Ironically, that drama put me on Kara's radar as she was the receiver of the Matchmaker's warnings. She went to my website and read one of my articles—a Mother's Day piece for single moms that spoke directly to what she was going through at the time. Then she read everything else I'd written.

Through our mutual friend Renee—Denice's sister—we got connected. We talked on the phone and agreed to meet for coffee. I told her up front, *"I'm looking for friends. If that changes, you'll be the first to know."*

There was something about her. I couldn't get her out of my prayers. I thought, *This woman is different.*

By our third meeting, I told her I was interested in dating her, with marriage in mind. We kept boundaries in place. I'd drawn the purity line years earlier, and I wasn't crossing it.

Thinking back, I used to be the guy who was never getting married again—and if I did, it certainly wouldn't be to someone I hadn't slept with. But all of that—the mindset, the fear, the "what ifs"—was gone. I had a clarity I'd never known before. I wasn't caught up in me or her. I was focused on what God had.

God's Confirmation

The confirmation didn't come through fireworks or a dramatic sign. It came one simple Saturday when Kara and I had planned to meet for lunch at my downtown loft. My oldest daughter, Taylor, happened to be in town that same day, and I suggested—almost casually—that maybe Kara would want to meet the girls. No pressure. Just lunch.

So Taylor and Sydney came over. Kara arrived shortly after. We ate, talked, laughed a little. Then the girls pulled out some old photo albums, flipping through memories and telling stories. And I just sat there watching it all unfold—these women I loved more than anything, sitting across from the woman God was stitching into my future.

And right there, something clicked:

I finally understood why dating had never felt peaceful.

No matter how much work God had done in me, there was still one thing I couldn't move past—I needed to know my daughters would be okay. Their future mattered in my future. Their hearts mattered in every decision I made. And without their peace, I never really had mine.

After Kara left, God gave me an unexpected confirmation. My youngest, Sydney—the same little girl who once looked up at me at three years old and asked, "Why are you and Mommy getting a divorce?"—turned to me and said, "I wouldn't mind if she were our stepmom."

That was the moment I recognized what God had already been doing. The door I'd been guarding finally opened—not because my daughter gave permission, but because God had been preparing my heart to trust Him with what came next. It was His quiet assurance: This is safe. This is good. You can move forward now.

We talked for the first time on June 25. Met in person on July 1. Started dating on July 15. Engaged by the end of October. Married by the end of December and moved into our new home right after.

All the preparation—financially, spiritually, emotionally—meant I could buy a house, pay for a ring and a wedding, and step into marriage without dragging the past in with me. With Kara, I gained not just a wife, but a son, a mother-in-law, brothers, and even a dog named Flash, who, by God's sweet detail, looked just like Max, my old dog who had died years before.

It felt like God had restored so much of what I had forfeited through my own choices.

My Conviction on Remarriage

What happened that day with the girls gave me peace on one level—their level. Their release mattered more than I ever admitted. But as much as I loved seeing their comfort with Kara, there was another layer I still had to face. The deeper one. The one between me and God.

Because long before Kara showed up, I'd been wrestling with a question that wouldn't leave me alone:

Was I even allowed to remarry?

This part of my story didn't come quickly or easily. It took years of prayer, Scripture study, and wrestling with God before I had peace about remarriage. And if you've been divorced and you love God, you've probably asked the same thing.

Religion—and especially Scripture taken out of context without the truth of God's grace—can make remarriage for someone like me—the unfaithful, the adulterer, the "bad one"—seem impossible. For a long time, I believed that. And believing it made me rebel.

But when I began to understand God's heart—not someone's misrepresentation of Scripture—I realized it was never about remarriage for me. It was about pleasing God.

My intention and heart became to honor Him, no matter the outcome. I had given up on marriage, sex, and all of it—in what most would call my prime—because pleasing God was more important. That's not a formula; it was just the truth for me. *Honor God first, and then all these things will be added* (Matthew 6:33).

The benefits of doing that far outweigh anything I can truly describe. To experience marriage as God intended, even with my jaded past, is an amazing thing. I get to serve my wife in the way that I believe God calls us to—because I am free. That freedom was God working out in me over the years of removing the things that didn't belong.

Here's what helped me settle it in my own heart:

1. **Understand God's Design.** Marriage was His idea. It's a covenant, not a contract. Breaking that covenant is never without cost, but God's redemptive heart is to heal and restore the broken.

2. **Examine Your Biblical Grounds.** Ask honestly: Was there sexual unfaithfulness? Was there abandonment by an unbelieving spouse? Were you the one who broke the covenant, or were you the one sinned against? God knows the truth, even if the details are messy.

3. **Seek Forgiveness.** Until you fully accept God's forgiveness for your part in the breakdown of your marriage, you will carry shame into your next relationship.

4. **Live a Season of Singleness With Purpose.** Let God do the deep work. For me, that meant years of refining—becoming emotionally stable, financially responsible, spiritually strong, and physically healthy before even thinking about marriage again.

5. **Invite Wise Counsel—But Don't Replace God's Voice With Theirs.** Godly friends and mentors can help you see blind spots, but they can't hear God's voice for you.

6. **Consider Your Children's Hearts.** Their peace matters too. Remarriage reshapes their world, even as adults. I couldn't move forward until I had peace that my daughters would be okay—not just with Kara, but with the idea of me marrying again.

In the end, I believe that remarriage is possible for anyone who has seen a genuine heart change toward Christ and away from selfishness, no matter their divorcing circumstances.

Why? Because in Christ, you are a new creation; the old is dead (2 Corinthians 5:17). If eternal life is possible simply by confessing with your mouth and believing in your heart (Romans 10:9), then you can trust God to redeem even this.

Remarriage can't be approached in selfishness. God is not a genie in a bottle waiting to grant your wish. He's a good Father who wants the best for His children, so much so that He'll let you walk away, but welcome you home when you return.

By the time Kara and I began dating, I had peace, not because she made me feel alive again, but because God had already settled the question long before I met her. She wasn't coming to fix me. God had already done the healing. She was a gift I could love without needing her to complete me.

For the One Wondering if It's Possible

If you're wrestling with remarriage, take it seriously. Wrestle with God over it. Get your Big Four in order. Let Him search your heart.

And when the time comes—whether God calls you to lifelong singleness or to remarriage—you can walk in it with peace, because you're not chasing completion in another person. You've already found it in Him.

And maybe, like me, you'll look back one day and realize that every step—every loss, every delay, every moment you thought nothing was happening—was God carefully piecing the story together.

Reflection Questions

- ⇒ What does God's timing look like in your story right now? Are you trying to rush or force something He's asking you to wait on?
- ⇒ How do you define "readiness" for a relationship? Does that definition come from culture or from God's refining work in you?
- ⇒ What fears or past wounds would you need to surrender before stepping into a new relationship or marriage?
- ⇒ Have you made peace with your past—not by rewriting it, but by letting God redeem it?

Practical Activity

Take an hour this week to sit quietly with God and reflect on the desires of your heart—especially around love, companionship, or marriage.

Ask Him honestly:

"God, what do You want to grow in me before You bring anyone to walk beside me?"

Write down what you sense He's saying. It might be a word, a phrase, or a reminder of something He's already shown you. Then thank Him for His timing—even if you don't understand it yet.

Prayer

> Father, thank You for knowing the desires of my heart—and for caring more about my wholeness than my hurry. Teach me to trust Your timing, even when it feels delayed. Help me release control and rest in Your wisdom. Whether You call me to marriage or to singleness, let my life reflect Your love and Your glory. Prepare my heart to love like You love—selflessly, patiently, and with grace. Thank You for redeeming what I thought was lost. Amen.

CHAPTER
18
WALKING INTO YOUR NEXT CHAPTER

If you've made it to this point, I believe something in these pages has reached you — maybe it challenged you, maybe it encouraged you, maybe it brought you face-to-face with God in a new way.

You've walked with me through the wreckage and rebuilding of my life — from the shock of divorce to the long road of healing, to the places where God restored what I thought was gone forever. You've seen the Big Four show up over and over — spiritual, emotional, physical, and financial health — because they don't just matter in one season; they hold you steady in all of them.

You've seen how God worked, not in an instant, but over years — through surrender, through people I didn't even know would become lifelong friends, through losses I didn't think I could survive, and through victories I never thought I'd see.

If I could tell you one thing here at the end, it's this: your story isn't over.

Not because you've read this book, and not because I'm telling you it will get better — but because God Himself says it's not over.

We've talked about shock and grief, about purity and surrender, about fatherhood and forgiveness. We've talked about letting go of pride, learning to live with purpose, and opening our hearts again. And I hope you've caught this truth along the way: the same God who met me in my lowest moments is already in your tomorrow, working all things together for your good.

I didn't believe that at first. I thought my life would be defined by failure. But now, looking back, I can see the quiet order He was bringing to the chaos — connections made years before I needed them, lessons that only made sense later, losses that shaped the man I'd become. He was writing a better story than I could have ever planned.

And He's doing the same for you.

The Invitation That's Still on the Table

If you've never placed your full trust in Jesus, I can't think of a better moment than right now.

He's the only One who can take away the weight of sin, the sting of shame, and the power of regret. He doesn't just clean up your past — He makes you new (*2 Corinthians 5:17*).

Salvation isn't about what you promise to do for God. It's about believing what He's already done for you — that Jesus died for your sins, was buried, and rose again, so that anyone who believes in Him will not perish but have eternal life (*John 3:16*).

The Bible says, *"If you confess with your mouth that Jesus is Lord and believe in your heart that God raised Him from the dead, you will be saved."* (*Romans 10:9*)

That kind of belief isn't just acknowledgment — it's trust. It's placing your hope, your life, and your eternity in the hands of the One who gave everything for you.

If that's what you want — if you're ready to stop trying to fix yourself and instead trust the One who can make you new — you can express that faith with a simple prayer like this:

A Prayer of Faith

Jesus, I know I've fallen short. I believe You died for my sins and rose again to give me new life.

I trust You — not my effort, not my goodness, not my religion.
Thank You for the gift of grace that I could never earn.
Come into my life, forgive me, and make me new.
Teach me to walk with You in faith and truth.
Amen.

If you prayed that, take a moment.

Breathe.

This isn't about perfection or performance — it's about believing that what Jesus did on the cross was enough.

Faith is simple, but it's not shallow. It's the beginning of a new life rooted in grace, one step at a time.

Your Next Step — The Prayer List Challenge

I want to leave you with something practical — a step you can take before you even close this book.

In 2020, I made a list of 300 specific things I asked God to do — for me, my friends, my family, and even for people I considered enemies. By the next year, God had already answered over half of them. Not all in the way I expected, but in ways that changed my heart, my relationships, and my future.

Here's why I believe this matters:

Prayer shifts our focus. It moves us from panic to trust, from hopelessness to expectancy. It aligns us with God's will. And it keeps us from settling for less than what He's promised.

Your challenge is simple:

➲ Make your own list — it doesn't have to be 300, but it should stretch your faith.

- Write down prayers in every area of your life — spiritual, emotional, physical, financial, relational.
- Be specific. The more clearly you can see the prayer, the more clearly you'll see when God answers it.
- Then pray over it every day.

Remember, you're in the request department, not the results department. God's timing is perfect, and His answers are always for your good.

Before you close this book, make your list. Stand on His Word. Ask boldly.

Jesus said in *Matthew 7:7-8*, *"Ask, and it will be given to you; seek, and you will find; knock, and it will be opened to you."*

Take Him at His Word. See if He doesn't change your situation, your mind, and your future. I believe He will — because His Word says so.

Reflection Questions

- What part of your story do you still need to place in God's hands?
- Where have you seen His restoration so far?
- What's one specific prayer you'll put on your list today?

Practical Activity

Make your prayer list today.
Write it. Pray it. Watch what God does.

Prayer

Father, Thank You for walking with me from the wreckage to this place of hope. Thank You for the thread of Your faithfulness woven through every page of my story. I give You my future. Align my steps with Yours. Grow my faith as I pray bold, specific prayers, and help me trust Your timing in every answer. I believe You will do immeasurably more than I could ask or imagine. In Jesus' name, Amen.

Stay Connected

If you're looking for what's next, visit **singlemanwalking.com**. There, you'll find resources, reflections, and encouragement to keep walking forward. You don't have to navigate this alone. Let this community walk with you, the way you've let this book walk with you.

ACKNOWLEDGMENTS

This book exists because I was not alone in the valleys—or in the rebuilding that followed. These words are for those who walked with me, prayed for me, challenged me, and stayed when things were heavy.

To James River Church, where God met me in seasons of brokenness and growth. For nearly two decades, this church was a place of transformation—where truth was spoken, grace was extended, and faith took root. Though God has led me into new seasons, I will always be grateful for the role this community played in my journey.

To the Crocker family, thank you for the ways you pointed me toward faith, even amid the complexities of our shared history. I honor the influence you had in my life and the lessons God used through you.

To Justin, your all-in faith and friendship have been a steady reminder that obedience and trust still matter. You've shown me what it looks like to believe God beyond what's visible, especially in seasons when I needed that reminder most.

To Jason, your friendship has shaped me more than you know. Walking through life, business, and hard conversations together taught me humility, honesty, and how to face conflict with grace. You've been a brother to me in every sense of the word. And to your wife and children—you've been family from the start.

To my mom, now with the Lord—I miss you more than words can hold. Your faith, joy, and love left a legacy that continues to anchor our family. I know you would be proud of the women my daughters have become. If I don't see you here, I'll see you in heaven.

To my daughters, Taylor and Sydney—being your dad is the greatest privilege of my life. You've taught me perseverance, presence, and unconditional love. You gave me reasons to keep showing up when quitting would have been easier. Some of the greatest joys of my life have come from being your dad.

To my wife, Kara—you are God's gift and kindness in my life. Your steadiness, encouragement, contagious joy, and love have strengthened me in ways I never expected. Walking forward together has been one of the clearest pictures of redemption I've known.

And finally, to God—thank You for staying when I wandered, lifting me when I fell, and redeeming what I could not fix. Every step forward has been sustained by Your grace.

ABOUT THE AUTHOR

George Lamelza doesn't write about divorce from theory or training—he writes from the wreckage of it.

After losing his marriage, home, and financial stability—and watching the business he built ultimately collapse—George spent years trying to outrun the pain before finally learning how to walk through it. The journey was slow, imperfect, and often uncomfortable—but it became the foundation for the story told in this book.

For more than five years, George has walked alongside men in divorce recovery settings, not as an expert with answers, but as someone who understands the confusion, loneliness, anger, and quiet fear that follow when life falls apart. His writing reflects that same posture—honest, grounded, and rooted in lived experience rather than formulas.

Professionally, George has spent nearly three decades in business, marketing, and technology. He's built and lost companies, navigated financial collapse, and rebuilt again—less concerned now with appearances and more focused on integrity, faith, and showing up well for the people who matter most.

George is a husband, father, and grandfather. At his core, he believes healing happens in stages, faith grows through surrender, and God wastes no broken story.

You can connect with George and find additional resources at SingleManWalking.com.